Corruption, Anti-Corruption and Governance

Political Corruption and Governance series

Series editors:

Paul M. Heywood is Dean of the Faculty of Social Sciences and Sir Francis Hill Professor of European Politics, University of Nottingham, UK.

Dan Hough is Reader in Politics and Director of the Sussex Centre for the Study of Corruption (SCSC) at the University of Sussex.

This series aims to analyse the nature and scope of, as well as possible remedies for, political corruption. The rise to prominence over the last 15 years of corruption-related problems and of the 'good governance' agenda as the principal means to tackle them has led to the development of a plethora of (national and international) policy proposals, international agreements and anti-corruption programmes and initiatives. National governments, international organisations and NGOs all now claim to take very seriously the need to tackle issues of corruption. It is thus unsurprising that over the last decade and a half, a significant body of work with a wide and varied focus has been published in academic journals and in international discussion papers.

This series seeks to provide a forum through which to address this growing body of literature. It will invite not just in-depth single country analyses of corruption and attempts to combat it, but also comparative studies that explore the experiences of different states (or regions) in dealing with different types of corruption. We also invite monographs that take an overtly thematic focus, analysing trends and developments in one type of corruption across either time or space, as well as theoretically informed analysis of discrete events.

Political Corruption and Governance series
Series Standing Order ISBN 978–113703457–1 (hardback) and 978–113703458–8 (paperback)

You can receive future titles in this series as they are published by placing a standing order. Please contact your bookseller or, in case of difficulty, write to us at the address below with your name and address, the title of the series and the ISBN quoted above.

Customer Services Department, Macmillan Distribution Ltd, Houndmills, Basingstoke, Hampshire RG21 6XS, England

Corruption, Anti-Corruption and Governance

Dan Hough
Professor of Politics, University of Sussex, UK

First published 2013 by
PALGRAVE MACMILLAN

Palgrave Macmillan in the UK is an imprint of Macmillan Publishers Limited, registered in England, company number 785998, of Houndmills, Basingstoke, Hampshire RG21 6XS.

Palgrave Macmillan in the US is a division of St Martin's Press LLC, 175 Fifth Avenue, New York, NY 10010.

Palgrave Macmillan is the global academic imprint of the above companies and has companies and representatives throughout the world.

Palgrave® and Macmillan® are registered trademarks in the United States, the United Kingdom, Europe and other countries

ISBN 978-1-137-26870-9

This book is printed on paper suitable for recycling and made from fully managed and sustained forest sources. Logging, pulping and manufacturing processes are expected to conform to the environmental regulations of the country of origin.

A catalogue record for this book is available from the British Library.

A catalog record for this book is available from the Library of Congress.

Contents

List of Tables		vi
Acknowledgements		vii
Note on the Author		ix
List of Abbreviations		x
Introduction		1
Chapter 1	The Rise and Rise of the Global Anti-Corruption Movement	12
Chapter 2	Governance Regimes and the Fight against Corruption	31
Chapter 3	Bangladesh and Kenya: Tough Talk, Small Steps, Ineffectual Outcomes	48
Chapter 4	South Korea and Poland: Tough Talk, Small Steps, Contested Outcomes	71
Chapter 5	Germany and the UK: The Slow and Winding Road to Reform	93
Conclusion		114
Notes		123
Bibliography		147
Index		162

List of Tables

2.1 Quality of governance and anti-corruption mechanisms 44
3.1 The quality of governance in Bangladesh, 1996–2002 50
3.2 The quality of governance in Kenya, 1996–2002 51
3.3 Control of corruption, Bangladesh, 1996–2010 52
3.4 Control of corruption, Kenya, 1996–2010 52
3.5 Bangladesh's performance in Transparency International's Corruption Perceptions Index, 2001–2011 54
3.6 Kenya's performance in Transparency International's Corruption Perceptions Index, 1998–2011 64
4.1 The quality of governance in South Korea, 1996–2002 73
4.2 The quality of governance in Poland, 1996–2002 74
4.3 Control of corruption, South Korea, 1996–2010 76
4.4 Control of corruption, Poland, 1996–2010 76
4.5 South Korea's performance in Transparency International's Corruption Perceptions Index, 1998–2011 78
4.6 Poland's performance in Transparency International's Corruption Perceptions Index, 1998–2011 86
5.1 The quality of governance in Germany, 1996–2002 95
5.2 The quality of governance in the UK, 1996–2002 96
5.3 Control of corruption, Germany, 1996–2010 98
5.4 Control of corruption, UK, 1996–2010 99
5.5 Germany's performance in Transparency International's Corruption Perceptions Index, 1998–2011 101
5.6 The UK's performance in Transparency International's Corruption Perceptions Index, 1998–2011 106

Acknowledgements

This book would not have seen the light of day if its author had not received the support and assistance of a number of people and from a number of institutions. Firstly, Amber Stone-Galilee at Palgrave Macmillan showed not just an enthusiasm for the project but also the willingness to support it until the bitter end! Paul Heywood, co-editor of Palgrave's Series on 'Corruption and Governance', has also been a constant source of support, encouragement and critical thinking. Both of them have played important parts in helping this book look like it does.

The University of Sussex did its utmost to help me both complete the research that underpins this book, and also to write up the findings, by allowing me to spend four months in late 2011 both out of the country and focused more or less completely on writing. The support, encouragement and particularly the enthusiasm of Paul Taggart has been really helpful in this regard. Other colleagues at Sussex have also regularly offered advice and constructive criticism, as well as their time in reading through various bits of the manuscript; Tim Bale in particular deserves a special note of thanks here. I am also extremely grateful to the German Academic Exchange Service (DAAD) who supported the early part of my research in Germany through their 'Study Visits for Academics' programme in November and December 2009.

Many of the ideas that have found their way in to what follows also came about thanks to input from my students at the University of Sussex. The undergraduate module on 'Political Corruption' that I have taught since 2004 has always been one of the most enjoyable parts of my job, and over the years students have regularly challenged me to think and re-think my own views on everything from how best to try and tackle corruption to what we should do about MPs' expenses claims. To all former students, particularly those who survived seminars in the now long-deceased Russell Building, I thank you! The first cohort of students on Sussex's MA in Corruption and Governance – Adrian, Anne, Ben, Ioannis, Malambo, Norbert, Paul, Ray, Sam, Sam and Sukri – also deserve a special word of thanks for the input they (sometimes inadvertently!) have had.

viii *Acknowledgements*

I would also like to thank all of the people I met at the Renmin University of China (RUC) in Beijing during my four month stay there in the Autumn of 2011; Lei Chen was always a model of efficiency in helping a frequently helpless 'lǎowài', whilst the almost never-ending stream of coffee that of all the girls (and William!) provided in the Law School Café played a pivotal role in keeping me going! I would also like to thank Professor He Jiahong – the law professor who also writes best selling crime novels – for all of his help before, during and also after my stay at RUC.

Given the way I lead my life – laptop in one hand, passport in the other (with cricket bat and football boots safely tucked in the backpack) – this book has actually been thought about, prepared and written in more places than most. The first chapter plans were penned somewhere over Russia on a flight from Heathrow to Guangzhou in April 2011, whilst the writing was set in train on warm, sun-filled days in my brother-in-law's flat in Liuzhou on that same trip. Various parts of the manuscript were written and tinkered with in a number of different branches of the Maan Coffee shop in China (RUC branch, please take note; they offer free refills at the Beijing Culture and Foreign Language branch, you know ...), as well as on train journeys from Clapham Junction to Brighton and at various other times on trips to Germany, the USA and Belgium. Again, various people helped massively along the way, reading things when nudged (or threatened!), and providing other means of support as and when required. With that in mind I would like to thank all of the following for showing an interest, commenting and criticising and generally just taking what I was trying to do at least a little bit seriously; Tom Guy, Grace and Pete Hough, Jonathan Olsen, and David Padgett. This book also wouldn't be my book if cricket didn't make a contribution somewhere – only this time it doesn't come anywhere in the text, but rather via the cover. With that in mind, many thanks to Twickenham CC stalwart Ben Parer for designing it!

Finally, there is one person whose support simply isn't quantifiable. And it is to her that this book is dedicated; my wife, Ying Lin.

University of Sussex,
September 2012

Note on the Author

Dan Hough is Professor of Politics and Director of the Sussex Centre for the Study of Corruption (SCSC) at the University of Sussex. Originally from Shropshire, he completed his undergraduate studies at the universities of Newcastle upon Tyne and Leipzig before moving to the Institute for German Studies at the University of Birmingham where he obtained his PhD in 2000. He then spent a year at the University of Nottingham before moving to the University of Sussex in 2003.

His research centres around political corruption, political parties and also issues of devolution and constitutional change. He has published two monographs (2002 and 2007, the latter co-written with Michael Koβ and Jonathan Olsen) on Germany's *Linke* (Left Party) and he has co-written two editions of the leading textbook in the field of German Politics (*The Politics of the New Germany*, 2008 and 2011, with Simon Green and Alister Miskimmon). He has published widely in referred journals such as *Party Politics, West European Politics, Journal of European Public Policy, Government and Opposition, Zeitschrift fuer Parlamentsfragen, Regional and Federal Studies* and *German Politics*.

When not working, Dan is likely either to be watching Shrewsbury Town Football Club or playing cricket for Twickenham CC. Or tweeting at @thedanhough

List of Abbreviations

ACA	Anti-Corruption Agency
ACECA	Anti-Corruption and Economic Crimes Act
ACPU	Anti-Corruption Police Unit (Kenya)
ACRC	Anti-Corruption and Civil Rights Commission (South Korea)
AGI	African Governance Indicators
AL	Awami League (Bangladesh)
BAI	Board of Audit and Inspection (South Korea)
BEEPS	Business Environment and Enterprise Survey
BNP	Bangladesh Nationalist Party
BPI	Transparency International's Bribe Payers Index
CCC	Committees of Concerned Citizens (Bangladesh)
CBA	Central Anticorruption Bureau (Poland)
CoE	Council of Europe
CPI	Transparency International's Corruption Perceptions Index
CPIA	Country Policy and Institutional Assessment
DEFRA	Department for Environment, Food and Rural Affairs (UK)
DWP	Department of Work and Pensions (UK)
EACC	Ethics and Anti-Corruption Commission (Kenya)
EU	European Union
FIU	Financial Intelligence Unit (Bangladesh)
FOI	Freedom of Information Act (UK)
GCB	Transparency International's Global Corruption Barometer
GCR	Global Competitiveness Report
GRECO	Group of States Against Corruption
IACC	Independent Anti-Corruption Commission (Bangladesh)
ICRG	International Country Risk Guide
IMF	International Monetary Fund
IMK	Standing Conference of Federal State Ministers and Senators of the Interior (Germany)

IPSA	Independent Parliamentary Standards Authority (UK)
K-Pact	Korean Pact on Anti-Corruption and Transparency
KACA	Kenya Anti-Corruption Authority
KACC	Kenyan Anti-Corruption Commission
KICAC	Korea Independent Commission Against Corruption
MoD	Ministry of Defence (UK)
NGOs	Non-Governmental Organisations
NHS	National Health Service (UK)
OACU	Overseas Anti-Corruption Unit (UK)
ODM	Orange Democratic Movement (Kenya)
OECD	Organisation for Economic Co-operation and Development
PCS	Parliamentary Commissioner for Standards (UK)
PiS	Law and Justice Party (Poland)
PNU	Party of National Unity (Kenya)
SFO	Serious Fraud Office (UK)
TI	Transparency International
TIB	Transparency International Bangladesh
UKBA	UK Bribery Act
UN	United Nations
UNCAC	United Nations Convention against Corruption
UNDP	United Nations Development Programme
UNESCAP	United Nations Economic and Social Commission for Asia and the Pacific
USAID	United States Agency for International Development
WEF	World Economic Forum
WGI	World Governance Indicators
YES	Youth Engagement and Support Groups (Bangladesh)

Introduction

Corruption is, it would appear, one of the great evils of our time. Citizens are appalled by it, international organisations have created reform agendas to tackle it and politicians earnestly claim to want to reduce it. Even the world of business has embraced the notion that it could well be in its interests to work alongside regulators and policy-makers with a view to cleaning up the environment where trade takes place, thereby eradicating bottlenecks in the system and by definition the costs that are incurred. Given the increased salience of corruption in the modern world, it comes as little surprise that in recent times social scientists have also conducted ever more analysis of corruption's underlying causes, its effects, and naturally what policy-makers have tried to do (and indeed should do in the future) to try and counteract it. Working to reduce the underlying negative effects of corruption therefore seems to be very much the order of the day.

And yet, as any student of politics in more or less any part of the world knows, these efforts have been at best only partially successful. Just turning the pages of any decent newspaper reveals as much. Indeed, one might quite plausibly come away with exactly the opposite impression – that things are getting worse, not better. News of corrupt acts comes thick and fast, and no sooner does one 'scandal' arrive than another appears to push it off the top of the agenda. Much of this may well be down to the rise of 24 hour news, the increasing effectiveness of investigative journalism and, indeed, the watering down of many of the bargains that underpinned political life during the Cold War era.[1] However, and in spite of everything,

1

there is certainly no concrete evidence to prove that politicians today are in fact any more or less corrupt than those of yesteryear. Yet perceptions of endemic corruption remain pervasive. Across the globe there is a systematic lack of faith in elected (or, indeed, unelected) public servants doing exactly what their name suggests; serving the public. These perceptions of widespread corruption hardly sit well with the apparent international consensus that corruption is an evil that must be slain wherever it is found. Where are things going wrong?

This book tries to answer that question. Although social scientists (and, indeed, politicians) have come a long way in terms of working out what, theoretically at least, should and shouldn't work in fighting corruption, we still have work to do in putting these theoretical insights into practice – into testing whether what actually happens matches our expectations. Or, put another way, under what conditions do which type of anti-corruption strategy work?

However, before that question can be answered, there are a number of important hoops to jump through. The first of these involves defining our terms. As has been amply illustrated in the literature, and as is the case with every contested concept, this is anything but easy. Even though definitions can generally be placed into one of three distinct categories – stressing the importance of public office, public interest or what have come to be known as 'market definitions' – international organisations still tend to use similar language;[2] Transparency International talks of 'the abuse of entrusted power for private gain', whilst the Organisation for Economic Co-operation and Development (OECD) believes corruption to be 'the active or passive misuse of the powers of public officials (appointed or elected) for private financial or other benefits'.[3] Christian Schiller, writing on behalf of the International Monetary Fund (IMF), believes corruption to be 'the abuse of public power for private benefit' although he also broadens this slightly by adding that it can be thought of as 'the abuse of authority or trust for private benefit'.[4] The World Bank, meanwhile, uses very similar language ('the abuse of public office for private gain'), whilst the Council of Europe shirks the challenge altogether by noting 'no precise definition can be found which applies to all forms, types and degrees of corruption or which would be acceptable universally'.[5] The Council of Europe is no doubt right, but in terms of conducting empirical research this truism isn't particularly helpful.

High-profile international organisations have not conjured their anti-corruption definitions and programmes out of thin air. On the contrary, the World Bank and IMF in particular have traditionally been keen to base their anti-corruption agendas on the evidence produced by (political or developmental) economists. It should not therefore be too much of a surprise that the most prominent analysis in this area largely concurs with the definitions employed by these organisations. Mushtaq Khan, for example, sees corruption as 'behaviour that deviates from the formal rules of conduct governing the actions of someone in a position of public authority because of private-regarding motives' whilst Arnold Heidenheimer et al. argue that it is a 'transaction between private and public sector actors through which collective goods are illegitimately converted into private-regarding payoffs'.[6] Andrei Shleifer and Robert Vishny, in more combative mode, argue that corruption is 'the sale by government officials of government property for personal gain'.[7] Susan Rose-Ackermann, in her seminal contribution from 1999, talks of the use of public office for 'private economic gain', whilst Robert Klitgaard sees corruption simply as 'the misuse of office for unofficial ends'.[8]

This is not to deny that definitions centring around the private gains made by public officials don't have their critics; Daniel Kaufmann, former head of the World Bank's Governance team and now of the Brookings Institute, talks for example of 'the privatisation of public policy', stressing how he feels traditional definitions place too much emphasis on public office and not enough on the role of the private sector in attempting to shape laws, regulations and agendas in their own interest.[9] Political anthropologists can also be fiercely critical of such definitions. They, too, are sceptical of the blind eye that can get turned to the corrupters, and particularly the assumption that the private sector is simply reacting to opportunity structures created by public officials when, of course, it might well be that public servants are being well and truly worked-over by skilful private actors.[10] Anthropologists have also repeatedly criticised what they claim is a very western understanding both of 'public office' as a concept and the notion of rational-legal bureaucracy more generally.[11] These ideas don't always travel at all well.[12] This leads on to one of the most enduring problems in defining corruption; ultimately, one's understanding of the corrupt will be indelibly linked with one's understanding of the political. One person's 'deal' is another person's 'corrupt act'. One person's 'gift' is another person's 'bribe'. Values, norms and ideas that shape your understanding of what politics actually is are therefore fundamental to understanding what is and isn't an acceptable part of the process.[13] This is all well and good, but it is no basis on which to go out and genuinely conduct comparative research. In order not to get dragged into definitional debates that can often appear to have no end, the following definition will suffice: corruption remains in essence the abuse of a public role for private gain.[14] This is not to say that context counts for nothing. In fact, context doesn't just matter, it is, as the following chapters reveal, absolutely vital in understanding how to move forward.

The second issue that those wishing to tackle corruption have to contend with is the politics of fighting corruption. Successful anti-corruption programmes rely on politicians building broader coalitions of support and also sticking with their policies in to the long-term. Whilst high-profile anti-corruption commissions or national campaigns to clean up public life may sound laudable and indeed be well intentioned, such initiatives all-too-often prove ineffective (and at times they can actually make problems worse) – especially if politicians can't carry respective stakeholders (i.e. civil servants, political opponents, civil society organisations and not to mention the citizenry) with them.[15] This is particularly true where the institutions of governance are not of a high quality and when deeply entrenched vested interests have the opportunity to resist.[16] Indeed, in such environments it may well be better to actually avoid talking directly about fighting corruption and to concentrate on more fundamental issues such as expanding or supporting the development of the rule of law or introducing a bill of rights. In other words, it may well be better to under-promise and over-perform. Getting at the key drivers of corruption needs a firm understanding of the local context; it takes time, and there are rarely quick and easy solutions to what are often deep-seated problems. Furthermore, even when the most blatant and obvious instances of corruption occur, there is rarely a consensus on what must be done to prevent such things happening again. The controversial position of the Independent Parliamentary Standards Authority (IPSA) in the UK following the expenses controversies that engulfed Members of Parliament in 2008 and 2009 is prima facie evidence of this.[17]

Tackling corruption: Ways forward

Before analysing the relationship between what can be termed 'governance regimes' and specific types of anti-corruption strategies and mechanisms, we begin in Chapter 1 by analysing the rise and development of the global anti-corruption industry. Chapter 2 moves on to analyse how the need to understand governance regimes and local opportunity structures became so important before illustrating how this book uses work on hypothesised linkages between governance and corruption to shape the empirical work in Chapters 3, 4 and 5. Whilst measuring governance is a process that is as fraught with difficulty as measuring corruption, there have been real advances in recent years and data such as those produced in the World Governance Indicators (WGI) can be useful starting points for conducting qualitative research on specific types of anti-corruption regime or policy, as well as on individual countries. Indeed, as Kaufmann et al. have commented, WGI composite indicators 'are useful as a first tool for broad cross-country comparisons and for evaluating broad trends over time' but they are often 'too blunt a tool to be useful in formulating specific governance reforms in particular country contexts'.[18] Furthermore, as Kaufmann et al. also note, 'such reforms and evaluation of their progress need to be informed by much more detailed and country-specific data' that help the researcher to 'identify the relevant constraints on governance in particular country circumstances'.[19] It is to precisely this challenge – the need to do theoretically informed analysis of indicative cases – that this book takes up.

Before explaining this book's approach in more detail, it makes sense to step back and analyse what we know about anti-corruption efforts thus far. There has unsurprisingly been a large rise in the amount of literature in this area in recent times.[20] The complexity and diversity of this literature – with contributions from a wide range of academic disciplines – illustrates just some of the problems that the policy community faces. And yet, until relatively recently, international organisations such as the World Bank and the IMF were very clear about what should be done to counteract corruption. This essentially involved embracing what came to be known as the 'lean government' agenda. The state – particularly in the developing world – was seen as being more or less inefficient and ineffective, and those working within it prone to abusing their positions of power and influence. Whilst it would be unfair to say that markets were seen as having the power to solve everything (corruption included), there was a sustained scepticism about the ability of governments (or those working in or for them) to avoid becoming embroiled in corrupt practices.[21] A number of the organisations that pushed corruption up their policy agenda in the 1990s – such as the World Bank and the IMF – subsequently bought in to much of the academic analysis that started from a clear public choice perspective; IMF economist Vito Tanzi, for example, claimed that the 'growth of corruption is probably linked with the growth of some of the activities of the government in the economy' subsequently arguing that reducing corruption will happen predominantly in states where 'government[s] are willing to substantially reduce some of their functions'.[22] The IMF itself claimed that 'corruption thrives in the presence of excessive government regulation and intervention in the economy' while the World Bank enthusiastically embraced the need to deregulate aspects of production as an important step towards reducing opportunities for corruption.[23] The state, in other words, and according to these organisations, needed to be restricted and restrained, and a culture of transparency and accountability introduced.[24]

While few people disagree with these last two points, a significant number of people were highly suspicious of the first. Privatising state functions, limiting the state's role and hiving off state activities may well fit particular sets of ideological agendas, but its empirical record in terms of fighting corruption is mixed at best.[25] In fact, as Hopkin and Rodriguez-Pose convincingly illustrate, 'advanced industrial nations, for the most part, have long intervened heavily in their economies while enjoying low levels of corruption' and 'the magnitude of government intervention in the economy in its broadest sense has little to do with corruption'.[26] Plus, of course, the least corrupt states (at least according to the bodies that claim to measure such things) do not appear to be those with the smallest public sectors and state apparatus – they tend to be the (much bigger) states of places like Sweden, Finland and Denmark.[27] Stiglitz's well known maxim that it is 'not so much that government is too big, but that it is not doing the right thing' would appear, then, to make a lot of sense.[28]

The rise of the governance agenda

Awareness that one-size-fits-all policy prescriptions are not the way forward has subsequently become more widespread. Indeed, the importance of understanding country-specific dynamics before recommending, let alone implementing, reform agendas is now a sine qua non of corruption analysis.[29] This change has gone hand in hand with the recognition that a country's governance regime will shape and impact on given anti-corruption mechanisms.

The term 'governance', of course, is not new. Indeed, interest in the art of governing dates back to the inception of Athenian democracy. However, through the 1990s a variety of international aid agencies and a range of international institutions from the United Nations Development Programme (UNDP) through to the World Bank, IMF, OECD and other development banks brought the term very much in to the mainstream by formally embracing what they described as 'governance agendas'.[30] Although there are many competing ways of defining what 'governance' means in practice, it is at root 'the traditions and institutions by which authority is exercised'.[31] In essence this involves looking at (and improving) a wide-range of policies spanning increased public accountability and transparency through to strengthening the rule of law, and from increased civil society participation in political life through to respect for human rights and the environment. Many international donors subsequently demanded that recipients of their largesse adopt what they – the donors – believe are approaches that lead to better governance.

Through the first decade of the 21st century more and more attempts have been made to quantify what 'good governance' actually looks like in practice. Daniel Kaufmann and his (former) colleagues at the World Bank have been arguably the most prominent scholars in the field, and they have consistently called for (and are themselves developing) more and better quality data on which to base such judgements. Indeed, they now publish data with the aim of generating 'snapshots' of a country's governance profile. The World Governance Indicators that Kaufmann has been prominent in developing provide an expansive dataset, refined over a number of years and comprising six aggregate indicators, to illustrate just how governance can and does change over time. They subsequently present detailed data on governance quality for (in 2010) 213 countries and territories.[32] Their analysis is revealing; as Kaufmann notes, the most powerful economies are not always the best governed.[33] However, Nordic countries and New Zealand do show that it is possible to achieve and maintain very high standards over a sustained period of time, whilst in 2010 over 30 countries performed better than long-standing EU members such as Italy and Greece.

Analysis of governance has subsequently come a long way in a short time. The picture on governance is nonetheless a highly nuanced one, even if some patterns across all six of the indicators Kaufmann et al. use – of which control of corruption is one – are evident.[34] States can do well in some areas but poorly in others, and Kaufmann et al. explicitly refuse to create league tables or even to make direct comparisons between countries. What they do stress, time and time again, is the need to understand a country's respective governance profile and to understand the causal mechanisms that have led to improvements or a worsening in governance quality.

Approach

This book uses these 'snapshots' as a guide to analysing the relationship between quality of governance, specific approaches to tackling corruption and reasons for their respective success or failure. In other words, the book analyses how and why a number of the policy prescriptions that this governance literature explicitly proposes pan out in practice. The book subsequently undertakes a qualitative analysis of anti-corruption mechanisms or approaches in six indicative cases, with a view to nuancing our understanding both of which anti-corruption approaches, strategies and methods appear to work best in which circumstances and concomitantly which do not.

Scholars have regularly talked of states as having 'poor', 'fair' or 'good' structures of governance and they have also pinpointed particular approaches and/or mechanisms that are likely to be more or less successful for each category. It is this framework that is used here.[35] To be more specific, the book analyses six countries that began the 21st century at broadly similar points on the governance spectrum; two perform relatively well in terms of quality of governance, two perform relatively poorly. Two are neither good nor poor but somewhere in between. For each of the cases the book looks at the anti-corruption approaches/mechanisms that are supposedly most applicable in tackling corruption in that context. In other words, we take the 'snapshot' as it was at the turn of the century and look to analyse whether, how and why each country has attempted (if indeed it has attempted at all) to tackle corrupt practices. In some cases the prescribed approaches have been relatively successful, in other cases less so. In some cases other mechanisms have been implemented, with mixed results. Given that the countries had broadly comparable governance regimes, adopting this approach enables us to get a feeling – over a ten year period – of how and why these successes and failures happened. Place-specific factors will obviously shape these outcomes too, but a detailed analysis of these specific anti-corruption attempts will nonetheless enable us to pinpoint more generalisable factors about that particular approach that may travel to other countries facing similar challenges. In other words, the book builds on well-established quantitative findings to offer qualitative depth and nuance.

Cases

In Chapters 3, 4 and 5 the book draws a series of paired comparisons. In terms of states with 'poor' governance records at the end of the 1990s/beginning of the 2000s, we take the cases of Bangladesh and Kenya. We view them as 'poor' based on the most recent set of WGI available (1996–2010). Although not identical (as no two governance profiles ever will be), a decade ago they did possess a number of distinct similarities. Although in 2000 Kenya performed better in terms of *government effectiveness* and particularly *regulatory quality*, Bangladesh had higher *voice and accountability* scores. Both, however, struggled in the bottom percentile in terms of *control of corruption, rule of law* and *political stability* (see Chapter 3).

Their less than glowing governance records were reflected in Transparency International's trademark Corruption Perceptions Index (CPI). In 2001 Bangladesh registered a meagre 0.9 whilst Kenya was on an uninspiring 2.0. However, by 2011 Bangladesh had improved its rating to 2.7 whereas Kenya's score had hardly moved (2.2). The CPI is meant only to give 'ball park' indications (i.e. one should not emphasise small differences in scores too much), but 'something' in Bangladesh was clearly working whereas that did not appear to be the case in Kenya. Given that the two states' respective governments had attempted to do broadly similar things, the book looks to see whether Bangladesh had implemented – and was benefiting from – what the literature hypothesises it should have, namely from doing one or a number of the following; reducing the size of the public sector, granting the media and judiciary more independence, reforming economic policy, increasing citizen participation in political and civic life and/or strengthening the rule of law. These moves, according to Jeff Huther and Anwar Shah at least, theoretically reduce potential for corruption by moving decision-making into the open and away from the hands of corrupt public servants whilst assisting interested parties (citizens, the media, other institutions) who seek to detect corrupt practices.[36] If they did indeed work, why did they not do so in Kenya? Data from the two cases is used to analyse these strategies, and then to make recommendations for other countries in similar situations.

Chapter 4 takes the same approach by analysing South Korea and Poland, both of which could, at the end of the 20th century, be categorised as 'fair' in terms of the quality of their governance. Poland appears to slightly outperform South Korea in terms of *voice and accountability* but South Korea does better in terms of *government effectiveness*. In other areas the profiles for the two states are similar. Both states also appear to have made progress in terms of their CPI scores; in 2001 South Korea registered 4.2 whereas Poland got 4.1. By 2011 both had made considerable improvements, South Korea moving up to 5.4 and Poland to 5.5. Again, the CPI numbers should not be taken as hard evidence, but they do indicate that something has improved noticeably in both states, and this book looks to pinpoint what exactly that was. The book aims to analyse to what extent these CPI scores correspond with reality on the ground by analysing the effects of the following; an increased emphasis on a merit based civil service, more parliamentary oversight, strengthening of media and judicial independence, the use of anti-corruption commissions, and a reduction in public sector size. As with the first paired comparison, we also investigate whether and how other policies have impacted on corruption.[37]

In terms of 'good' governance categories, we look at the UK and Germany. Although the UK lagged (and continues to lag) behind Germany in terms of *political stability*, the two countries look very similar indeed in terms of the other six indicators. Yet in 2001 the UK found itself scoring 8.3 in the CPI whereas Germany registered a score of 7.4. By 2011, these roles had again been reversed, the UK slipping 0.5 points (to 7.8), whereas Germany had improved by 0.6 points (to 8.0). Here, we again take a broad view but we are particularly interested in whether explicit anti-corruption laws and programmes have had an impact, high-profile convictions have been secured and whether accountability processes have been strengthened. Such reforms should, in theory at least, increase accountability and processes of integrity management as public servants become (more) aware that their principals are paying greater attention to their work, whilst putting high profile miscreants on trial should not only raise awareness but also send out clear messages that everyone is equal in front of the law. The analysis here will add a rich, qualitative dimension to a debate that is traditionally dominated by quantitative analysis. And the conclusions will have far-reaching implications for policy-makers in nation-states and beyond.

1
The Rise and Rise of the Global Anti-Corruption Movement

Corruption has been around since time immemorial, but systematic attempts to try and counteract it have not. On the contrary, what its supporters often call the 'global anti-corruption movement' and critics the 'anti-corruption industry' is a relatively new phenomenon. Indeed, it may well be possible to pinpoint the birth of cross-national attempts to co-ordinate analysis of, and responses to, corruption to one date; the 1st of October 1996. Not that attempts to tackle corruption started precisely then, but when James Wolfensohn, the then head of the World Bank, stood up and gave a speech denouncing what he termed the 'cancer of corruption', it became clear that for the international policy community tackling corruption was moving centre-stage.[1]

Given that corruption is an age-old problem, why did it take so long for policy analysts to wake up to the challenge that it poses? And once tackling corruption did start to be taken seriously, what prescriptions did those who were concerned about corruption come up with? This chapter illustrates that whilst anti-corruption certainly 'arrived' in the 1990s, its path to centre stage was not without controversy. Although a consensus was quickly established across much of the international policy community as to what the key drivers of corrupt practices were, and subsequently what should be done to snuff them out, by the early 2000s a strong lobby was developing that felt not only that these anti-corruption methods and approaches were not working, but, even worse, they were in many ways detrimental to the cause and, for some, bordering on the self-serving.[2] The anti-corruption movement has subsequently found itself forced to reassess much of what it treated, through the 1990s, as self-evident common sense, questioning its own assumptions, ideological underpinnings and, subsequently, methods and strategies. This chapter illustrates that influential though many of the international organisations (and the policies that they espouse) remain, anti-corruption attempts in the second decade of the 21st century are now much more nuanced and flexible than they were just a few years previously.

(Anti-)corruption: The dog that could barely raise a whimper

As has been widely discussed elsewhere, corruption and anti-corruption were off political scientists' respective radars for much of the 20th century. Indeed, as Michael Johnston has observed, 'American political science as an institutionalised discipline has remained steadfastly uninterested in corruption for generations'.[3] Political science was, however, not alone in its neglect of corruption and the studies that were produced tended to be few and far between. Through the 1950s and 1960s, for example, a group of developmental economists did begin to analyse the role that corruption was playing in the newly independent states of Africa and parts of Asia. With the advent both of independence and in many cases democratisation there was an assumption that these states would eventually increase in prosperity and come to move down a path of what – for better or worse – was termed modernisation. By the 1960s, however, it became clear that many states were either making painfully slow progress or were not on this path at all. Endemic corruption was seen as just one part of the explanation for this and a group of authors subsequently started to analyse not just how corruption was hindering development but also how, for some at least, it may also offer help in jump starting stagnant economies and hence a way forward.[4]

The debates of the 1960s none the less had something of a patronising feel about them. Corruption was seen as 'symptomatic of a "backward" level of political development' or of an inability to 'modernise' effectively.[5] Given that the western world was long since believed to have grown out of such behaviour, corruption was subsequently seen as something that 'immature societies' suffered from; indeed, in the words of Samuel Huntington, 'when the leaders of juntas and revolutionary movements condemn the "corruption" in their societies, they are, in effect, condemning the[ir states'] backwardness'.[6] For political anthropologists in particular, these positions simply were not tenable and a considerable body of literature built up with the aim of refuting what they saw as such culturally skewed analyses. Their aim was certainly not to defend the antics of anti-democratic leaders and the at times deplorable behaviour of some of the developing world's politicians, but, they argued, a little context was vital in understanding the processes and structures that corruption was flourishing in. The core tenets of this fight back were succinctly articulated by Elizabeth Harrison when she observed that 'comprehension of how opportunities are shaped, both to engage in and to escape from corruption, is important' before acerbically adding that unfortunately 'it seldom occurs'.[7]

Political scientists only really entered the fray in the late 1980s and the early 1990s. The reasons for this are threefold. Firstly, a move towards a more probing style of investigative journalism led both to more corruption scandals being uncovered and subsequently the (western) public's attention being drawn to them. Indeed, no western country was spared the phenomenon of at least a small number of prominent politicians being drawn into – frequently very unedifying – stories of grand or petty corruption.[8] Secondly, and linked with this, public and academic discourse began to change. Rather than write off individual indiscretions as the actions of the odd bad apple, citizens (and academics) began to ask if something in contemporary society was fundamentally flawed. Was there something corrosive about modern capitalism and, if so, what can and/or should be done about it? Finally, the end of the Cold War prompted not only changes in the way the West dealt with corrupt 'friends' in places like Indonesia, the Philippines and a whole host of African states but also how it approached the idea of institution-building in central and eastern Europe.[9] How, in other words, could newly democratising states avoid importing corrupt practices when developing their own institutional frameworks?

Once the academic floodgate was opened, then the trickle of articles and books that we had seen in the 1980s became, in the 1990s, a veritable torrent.[10] And it was here that the move towards an 'anti-corruption movement' gathered momentum. If former World Bank head James Wolfensohn's description of corruption as a cancer marked a sea change, then the creation of Transparency International (TI) in 1993 marked a critical juncture along the way to this point. In particular, TI's Corruption Perceptions' Index (CPI), launched in 1995, has played 'a pivotal role in focusing attention on corruption'[11] and even those with (often strong) reservations about the methodology that underpins it acknowledge the role that the organisation itself has played in pushing corruption on to national and international policy agendas.[12]

Transparency International and the quantification of corruption

Transparency International was founded by Peter Eigen, a former employee of the World Bank. TI has risen from relatively humble beginnings to become a complex organisation, with a yearly budget in the range of €9/10m, more than 90 national chapters and a well-staffed secretariat in Berlin.[13] Each national chapter enjoys considerable independence and can subsequently look and act quite differently.[14] As an organisation, TI itself is now the major force in pushing issues of anti-corruption forward.

TI's most well-known product remains the Corruption Perceptions' Index (CPI), published yearly in November/December. The CPI is a composite index and a variety of other data sources are used to create what is in effect a poll of polls on perceptions of corruption in a given country. Data is gathered from surveys of business people and country experts with the aim of measuring 'perceptions … of corruption in the public sector including corruption involving public officials, civil servants or politicians'.[15] TI provides a detailed account of where its data comes from and also how it uses it, and this is accessible via TI's own website.[16] The CPI was first published in 1995 and it included 41 countries, with New Zealand achieving the best score (i.e. nearest to 10) and Indonesia the worst (nearest to 0). By 2011 the CPI had expanded to 183 countries, with New Zealand still at the top of the pile (although it had been joint first in 2010 alongside Denmark and Singapore) and North Korea and Somalia respectively registering the lowest scores.[17] The data produced is used, in varying ways and for varying purposes, by journalists, other anti-corruption organisations and not least politicians, and the CPI has developed into the key brand name in the study of corruption worldwide.

The CPI's prominence has certainly not shielded it from criticism. Indeed, criticising the methodology that underpins the CPI has become very commonplace. Andersson and Heywood, for example, see a number of basic problems. Firstly, the CPI measures perceptions of corruption rather than corruption itself. Secondly, there are fundamental definitional problems leading us to be very unsure of what respondents actually understand the term corruption to mean. Indeed, frequently it appears that the terms bribery and corruption are used interchangeably and are for many one and the same thing. Thirdly, the CPI suffers from 'false accuracy' and there is no way of knowing what the real difference between scores that are closely grouped together is in practice. A difference, in other words, of just a few decimal places can lead to countries being a fair distance apart in the league table and yet we are not at all sure that these differences actually reflect what is happening in the real world. Finally, responses to the various surveys are very likely to be shaped by – whether directly or indirectly – the assumptions and attitudes of the western business community; for the simple reason that the majority of people asked have roots in this particular milieu.[18]

Other analysts have also not been slow in coming forward with their criticisms. Steve Sampson, speaking for many in the development studies community, is sceptical of what he regards as 'corruption becoming a scientific concept' as measurement tools like the CPI can, and have, easily become objects of political manipulation.[19] Even fellow quantifiers such as Stephen Knack and Anwar Shah from the World Bank have criticised some of the statistical techniques that TI have employed.[20] Indeed, Shah and Theresa Thompson leave no one in any doubt as to how grave they think the CPI's methodological shortcomings are when they state that 'closer scrutiny of the methodology ... raises serious doubts about the usefulness of aggregated measures of corruption' and 'potential bias introduced by measurement errors lead to the conclusion that these measures are unlikely to be reliable, especially when employed in econometric analyses'.[21] Knack's careful dissection of the CPI also makes uncomfortable reading for TI defenders; he argues, for example, that no eastern European or central Asian state's score in

2005 was based on the same set of sources that were used in 2004. This is evidence, he claims, of the unreliability of scores even within one country, let alone on a cross national basis.[22] He also raises further significant issues about the independence – in a statistical sense – of the data used, claiming that many of the 'statistically significant' changes that TI claims to have uncovered would not in reality be so if 'appropriate corrections for interdependence' had been made.[23]

For its part, TI has certainly tried its level best both to be open about the methodological shortcomings of the CPI (as well as its other corruption indices) and also to adjust them wherever possible. The founder of the CPI index, Johann Graf Lambsdorff, for example, is careful to acknowledge some of the methodological issues inherent in *all* composite indicators and he is always careful to describe changes in country scores from year to year as changes in *perceived* corruption rather in actual corruption levels.[24] TI has also tacitly admitted that the CPI has its limitations by the very fact that it has developed a whole host of other indices – such as the Bribe Payers Index and the Global Corruption Barometer – looking at both the perceptions and experiences of specific groups of stakeholders (ranging from businessmen to households).[25] One of TI's founders, Jeremy Pope, has been rather more explicit, claiming that 'the CPI's major usefulness is in the past' and the TI has to be 'a lot more sophisticated these days'.[26]

And yet, all these criticisms not withstanding, the CPI has done one indisputable thing; it has put the issues of corruption and anti-corruption well and truly on the policy map.[27] Indeed, as Andersson and Heywood observe;

> We should not underplay its significance in the fight against corruption: its value goes beyond the stimulation of research activity, since the publication of the CPI each autumn has generated widespread media interest across the world and contributed to galvanising international anti-corruption initiatives, such as those sponsored by the World Bank and the OECD.[28]

Even staunch critics of the quantification of corruption have begrudgingly admitted that 'whatever its limitations' the development of the CPI has 'undoubtedly done much to promote the anti-corruption agenda'.[29] It is also doubtful that any of the more nuanced second (and soon to be third) generation indices that both TI itself and other organisations have developed would have seen the light of day if the CPI hadn't existed before them.[30]

As indicated above, TI has been at the forefront of generating more sophisticated 'second generation' indices. Given the methodological challenges inherent in creating broad indices, the emphasis has shifted towards greater detail rather than increased breadth. Subsequently we now have indices looking at, amongst other things, state capture, the (legal and illegal) influence of the lobbying industry and the quality of the business environment. The WGI (see Chapter 2) are a fundamental part of this, just as are TI's own Global Corruption Barometer (GCB) and Bribe Payers Index (BPI). The development of the GCB in 2003 was a clear response to criticism of the CPI as too elite focused. The GCB is a public opinion survey that in 2010 asked over 91,000 citizens in 86 countries whether and how often they themselves have experienced what they regard as corruption.[31] The intention of the GCB is to bring ordinary people in to a field where their experiences and perceptions have traditionally been neglected. The BPI, meanwhile, looked specifically at incidences of bribery in (in 2008) firms from 22 'top exporting countries that account for roughly 75 per cent of total Foreign Direct Investment (FDI) outflows and export goods worldwide' and includes interviews with almost 3,000 senior business executives who were, at the time, working in 26 different countries.[32] The intention of the BPI is to link the real world experience of those who do business across national borders with one single, easily definable act (i.e. bribery). These second generation indices clearly illustrate that TI is attempting to move with the times; they provide individual-level indicators and there is much less chance of measurement error. They also, importantly, allow for specific margins of error to be recorded.[33] They are, in other words, much better tools for working out what really is going on in the real world.

TI's indices are, of course, not by any means the only game in town and the burgeoning survey landscape is testament to how important measuring corruption, or aspects of it, has become. A number of other organisations, for example, have tried to nuance our understanding of corruption's relationship to business. In 1999, 2002, 2005 and 2009 the 'Business Environment and Enterprise

Survey' (BEEPS) investigated the experiences of (over 11,000 in 2009) businessmen (in 29 countries) with corruption in eastern Europe and central Asia, while in 2005 the World Economic Forum (WEF) asked more than 10,000 firm managers similar sets of questions.[34] The WEF has also included several corruption-related questions in the 'Global Competitiveness Report' (GCR) (spanning 117 countries) whilst the Institute for Management Development adopts a very similar methodology to the GCR even though the questions it asks are slightly different.[35]

At the level of ordinary citizens, it is not just TI that has sought to probe deeper into the individual experience of corrupt practice. The World Values Survey now asks a number of questions on corruption, as do a number of the regional barometer surveys. The International Crime Victimisation Survey also asks whether government officials had demanded bribes for the services they provided over the previous 12 months.[36] Expert assessments also continue to be popular tools of choice; the World Governance Assessments have asked 35 apparent experts 30 questions (including three that pertain directly to corruption) and their data covers 16 countries. UNECA's Africa Governance Indicators (AGI) also embrace experts' panels with the panels varying in size from around 70 people to 120 and the International Country Risk Guide (ICRG) also conducts surveys of those it perceives to be experts in risk analysis.[37]

In summary, data on corruption is now in abundant supply and it has made a significant contribution to the policy analysis of international organisations interested in tackling corruption. Although multi-dimensional indicators are clearly problematic in some respects, Sampson's claim that 'the reliability of tools or other methodological issues are never totally brought out' is clearly unfair.[38] Those who are fundamentally sceptical of any attempt to define, let alone measure, corruption may not like the turn towards quantification, but it is unreasonable to claim that these organisations think they are dealing in an exact science. All of the organisations that produce indices (no matter whether they deal with perceptions or experiences of corruption) point out, to greater or lesser extents, the weaknesses in their respective approaches. They may have a fundamentally positivist view of the world, but this doesn't make them boffins who have no concept of the world's complexity. TI and other organisations in the data-producing field may, in other words, talk up their respective efforts to quantify aspects of corrupt practice (and who can blame them), but they do also realise that they are dealing in imperfections.

From measurement to the anti-corruption industry

The exponential rise in the number of organisations attempting to measure corruption has gone hand-in-hand with a much increased profile for what Bryane Michael describes as the 'anti-corruption industry', Ed Brown and Jonathan Cloke deride as the 'international crusade against corruption' and what Steve Sampson simply calls 'anti-corruptionism'.[39] Whatever one thinks of the merits of the enterprise, incorporating measures to tackle corruption certainly became a fundamental part of the aid and development strategies of many international organisations, think-tanks and indeed government departments. Undoubtedly, anti-corruption rhetoric and policy has long since become evident in thinking on ethics, governance, socio-economic policy, public administration and a whole range of other areas. Being encouraged to fight corruption is now so self-evidently a 'good thing' that it is incorporated either directly or indirectly into virtually all national and international public policy discourse.

Non-governmental organisations (NGOs) such as TI have done an impressive job of raising awareness but the international policy environment has been shaped mainly by international finance organisations such as the World Bank and the IMF, as well as the United Nations (UN), Organisation for Economic Cooperation and Development (OECD), the Council of Europe (CoE), the European Union (EU) and last but not least the United States.[40] And these organisations have not been scared to put their money where their respective mouths are; Bryane Michael and Donald Bowser estimate (conservatively, in their minds) that the size of the industry rose from roughly $100m in 2003 to around $5bn in 2009.[41]

Bryane claims that the anti-corruption industry has developed in three distinct but at times over-lapping 'waves'. More specifically, he talks of an initial wave of anti-corruption activity becoming apparent in the early 1990s. Awareness raising activities tended to be most prominent during this period, whether they be 'speeches, international conferences and even rock-concerts' and in financial terms they were generally supported (directly or indirectly) by organisations such as USAID (United States Agency for International Development) and the World Bank. A second wave developed in the late 1990s and early 2000s with most of the anti-corruption projects focusing 'primarily on capacity building'. Again, USAID and the World Bank were prominent, tendering large projects for which private charities, other groups that Michael describes as 'Beltway Bandits', and even star-individuals applied. A secondary market of anti-corruption service providers also developed at this time, as civil servants in many western countries moved from being 'expert advisors' on good practice to being 'contract managers and intermediaries for an army of "expert" consultants'.[42]

Finally, a third wave developed that centred around pragmatic, bilateral relationships. Michael argues that this era is characterised by the development of the EU into a key player in the anti-corruption industry 'with work done by actual boot-wearing law enforcement officials instead of eye-glass wearing graduate students and social science professors'. Michael points to the launch of a plethora of EU special missions with specific anti-corruption mandates as well as US policy moving 'away from policy-by-proxy funding mechanisms (using USAID, OECD and World Bank "partnership") in favour of pragmatic, targeted programmes' through agencies such as the US Department of Justice, Homeland Security and even the FBI.[43] Furthermore, Michael argues that this 'third wave' is characterised by a shift from '(often large-scale) procurements awarded to large consulting companies' towards direct co-operation between specific agencies. He claims that 'the superstar consultants of the late 1990s' are now much fewer and farther between and we 'see many Swedish and British police and customs officers roaming around eastern European capitals flogging their anti-corruption ware'.[44]

The global fight against corruption is therefore not only one where a lot of money is spent, it is one that employs a considerable number of people to come up with implementation strategies, think pieces, policy papers and review documents with the aim of helping specific actors reduce corruption levels. The cynics may argue that it is at times 'difficult to tell whether activists … are motivated by conviction, material benefits or both' but this would seem – as cynicism often does – to miss the point.[45] Many of the actors involved (including self-declared grassroots-orientated NGOs) are perfectly at home at the top tables of high politics. That, however, is not the problem; the real issue is the lack of impact and the painful reality is that, for all the funding, all the planning, all the organising, there is precious little evidence that the anti-corruption industry has systematically helped to mitigate the impact (let alone weed out the root causes) of corruption in everyday life. As Steve Sampson has astutely observed, 'despite hundreds of millions of dollars, and hundreds of programmes, projects, and campaigns, conducted by an army of anti-corruption specialists, experts, and trainers, we have very little evidence of any decline in corrupt behaviour'.[46] Daniel Kaufmann has gone even further, claiming that there is a 'silent crisis' as the anti-corruption movement appears unable to 'make the transition from the awareness-raising stage' to what he describes as the 'concrete action-orientated stage'.[47] Put another way, where breakthroughs have happened and where progress in specific country settings has been made, it appears more often than not that coincidence and place-specific influences have been every bit as important as anti-corruption strategies mandated by external bodies.

This is all rather depressing – not least because of the sums of money that have been invested but more pressingly because of the seriousness of the problem – and it begs the question 'where are we going wrong'? One partial answer to this is evident if one steps back and looks at the intellectual basis of many of the policies developed. The anti-corruption industry obviously comprises a diverse set of actors with diverse sets of ideas, beliefs and modes of operation. However, a significant part of this industry bought – at least until relatively recently – in to sets of ideas that, when one dissects them, were always likely to be less than opportune for achieving the grand goals set.

Linking practice and theory

If in practical terms James Wolfensohn's 1996 speech marked an important step towards prioritising 'anti-corruptionism', then the groundwork for how this would be implemented was already being done in the hallowed halls of academia. And this groundwork led to very specific sets of policy recommendations being developed. Through the 1990s in particular, a strong core of political economists developed a body of anti-corruption principles that soon morphed into anti-corruption policies. A number of the key actors in this debate had feet in both the policy and the academic camps – Susan Rose-Ackerman, for example, was (and still is) a distinguished scholar at Yale as well as for a time being a visiting research scholar at the World Bank, whilst Vito Tanzi had an academic background at both American and George Washington universities before becoming director of the IMF's department of fiscal affairs. It should subsequently come as little surprise that when international organisations, prompted by Wolfensohn's rallying call, began to discuss corruption then the ideas and recommendations of such thinkers gained particular resonance.

What did this mean in practice? Firstly, the academic analysis of corruption experienced what Jonathan Hopkin has described as an 'economic turn', as economists took ever more interest in questions of what caused corruption and what should be done about it.[48] Much of this analysis started from a position that was highly critical not just of the state's ability to efficiently and effectively deliver public goods but that also embraced a set of 'behavioural assumptions' that fundamentally distrusted politicians in the first place.[49] In essence, politicians – much like all human beings – were understood to be rational, self-interested, utility maximisers.[50] This led some analysts to be crystal clear that 'government intervention in the economy' is the root cause of corrupt practices[51] and 'a large government increases corruption and rent-seeking'.[52] Even the less fundamentalist strain of this 'public choice' approach to analysing political affairs was still unambiguous in claiming that 'excessive state intervention' would, sooner or later, directly or indirectly, lead to 'a range of ill-defined pathologies, ranging from low-level inefficiencies, through bureaucratic "shirking", to out-and-out corruption'.[53] For its most enthusiastic proponents there was not only a highly sceptical attitude towards the state but also a deeply held belief that firms and private enterprise more generally only indulged in corrupt transactions as they were either meeting the demands of corrupt bureaucrats or forced to do so on account of overwhelming state regulation. As Ninghua Zhong, a true believer, states 'the demand for corruption mainly comes from the will of firms to reduce costs associated with government regulations or to obtain opportunities to enter into regulated markets'.[54] There is no, or very little, apparent thought that these firms may – at least theoretically – also be seeking to manipulate the environment for their own ends so that policies can be developed and implemented that suit their own sets of interests.

For many scholars who embraced this approach, corruption analysis subsequently offered an opportunity not just to illustrate that the state was wasteful but also that the rent-seeking tendencies of politicians could, and indeed would, lead to an escalation in the number of corrupt practices.[55] Few went as far as Nobel Laureate Gary Becker in claiming that 'if we abolish the state, we abolish corruption'[56] but the idea that the state could provide efficient and effective (and by definition corruption-free) services was dismissed as idealistic 'romanticism'.[57] 'Corruption' in other words 'will be reduced mainly in those countries where governments are willing to substantially reduce some of their functions'.[58] Susan Rose-Ackerman's 1999 work provides the most emblematic example of this, as whilst the book has a number of eminently sensible suggestions for limiting incentives to act in a corrupt manner – keeping tax systems both simple and transparent, avoiding over-regulation that may prompt firms to 'cut corners' (i.e. bribe their way round them) – many of the suggestions are implausible in states that do not have strong, well-organised, legitimate and effective states policing them. Creating, for example, 'strong apolitical regulatory bodies' whose work is shaped by 'transparent and open processes' is a task that states with high levels of corruption are, by definition, unlikely to be able to fulfil. Rose-Ackerman herself claims that for effective regulation to function then a 'stable legal environment and credible enforcement institutions' are vital. Again, these may well be to hand in low-corruption countries, but in parts of the world where anti-corruption agendas are most needed they are most unlikely to exist.[59] And, as Hopkin notes, the public choice school from which much of this literature comes actually regards – on account of their specific understanding of human nature – these aims as impossible anyway.[60]

The fact that the data on the relationship between levels of public spending and incidences of corruption remains ambiguous did not stop many of the policy prescriptions from this school of thought from taking hold. State intervention in economic and social life was viewed increasingly sceptically and should subsequently be restricted to a set of specific, limited activities. In practice, this was seen to mean preserving law and order and upholding a clear and transparent legal system, protecting property rights, and providing only the most essential public goods that the market could not provide. In essence, these could be restricted to 'basic preventive health care, elementary education and national defence'.[61] Market mechanisms would efficiently and effectively allocate resources in all other areas. The fact that some (although not all) countries that spent disproportionately large amounts of money on public services could have low levels of corruption whilst some (although again not all) states that spent comparatively little had high levels of corruption was for the most part ignored. The assumptions that underpin much of this research were still upheld and adhered to. That this found resonance in many quarters of the US establishment in particular should not really come as too much of a surprise; 'the more pervasive is the public sector's role' argued Jim Saxton, the Republican New Jersey Congressman who authored a congressional report on the impact of IMF lending on corruption, 'the more likely corruption is to flourish'.[62] Despite the catchiness and inherent plausibility of the idea, the relationship clearly is not as simple as that and the subtle shades of grey that are evident in the real world tended to be either overlooked or explained away as deviant cases. This becomes evident when the programmes and policies of international organisations active in this field are put under the microscope.

International organisations and the anti-corruption agenda

The first international organisation to talk about corruption publicly was the United Nations (UN), and it did so well before the anti-corruption industry came on the scene. The UN's General Assembly adopted a resolution calling for international co-operation against corruption and bribery in international commercial transactions as early as 1975, although given that other institutions failed to follow this lead the resolution remained very much a paper tiger. It took fully 20 years for calls to be made for another resolution, this time for deeper and more sustained co-operation in halting the bribery of foreign officials – something that in many countries could still actually be written off for tax purposes. Eventually, the 'United Nations Declaration against Corruption and Bribery in International Commercial Transactions' was passed as the international community sought to pursue its development goals by opening up new, cleaner, more efficient channels of international commerce.[63] Following the 1996 breakthrough the UN regularly passed resolutions imploring member states to do more to fight corruption (and particularly bribery). While the UN resolutions were always careful to talk about the importance of maintaining and improving welfare standards for ordinary people, the logic behind the resolutions was still clear; creating efficient market mechanisms was the way not just to generate wealth, it was also the way to achieve broader goals of development and corruption prevention.

The practical effects of the UN's resolutions have remained relatively small, mainly as the UN does not have the tools to enforce (or even monitor) its own anti-corruption efforts. The same might be said of the OECD as it too started to think rather more about the impact of corruption. In the OECD's case, the US government was keen to persuade it (and subsequently other countries) to develop agreements that built on the USA's own 'Foreign Corrupt Practices Act' of 1977 (which prohibits American companies from bribing foreign officials). American willingness to level the playing field and stop its own companies from being in a disadvantageous position in relation to firms from elsewhere (who were implicitly still allowed to bribe) was certainly one reason for the development of the OECD's 'Convention on Combating Bribery of Foreign Public Officials in International Business Transactions' that was adopted in November 1997.[64] The convention requires signatories (of which at the time of writing there are 38) to enact domestic legislation criminalising the bribery of foreign public officials and to impose strong sanctions on those who break the law. The influence of the US in promoting the convention was not insignificant, but if it this were simply an American policy railroaded on to the international agenda then it is unlikely that the Americans would have taken fully two decades to bring the convention to fruition; indeed, the fact that there was a growing consensus across a range of influential NGOs and academics (principally economists) that corruption was impeding economic growth as well as development more generally also played a significant role.[65]

Whilst the influence of a discrete agenda is evident in the development of specific anti-corruption frameworks in the UN and OECD, it has been much more explicit – and much more clearly linked to the same set of assumptions that guide academics working in the public choice school – in both the IMF and World Bank. From the mid-1990s IMF-linked scholars began publishing working papers and academic journal articles arguing that corruption had a negative influence on a range of economic indicators such as growth and investment.[66] Furthermore, by September 1996 the IMF had developed a 'Partnership for Sustainable Global Growth' where tackling corruption was seen as an 'essential element of a framework within which economies can prosper'.[67] Furthermore, Mlada Bukovansky claims that since 2002 'more than half of the Fund's Public Information Notices have contained explicit references to governance or corruption' and 'over two thirds of the Letters of Intent, where country authorities describe their economic policies to the Fund, mention corruption'.[68]

It would be disingenuous to claim that the IMF's much increased interest in corruption was ill-conceived; clearly it is not, and the IMF and scholars closely linked to it are right to point to the array of damaging economic effects that corruption brings with it.[69] The IMF's mandate and resources also demand that it analyse corruption purely through the prism of whether, and how, it impacts on macroeconomic performance. However, the default positions of many IMF scholars – the more the state does, the more likely it is to foster corrupt activity – do come through when one scratches under the surface. Christian Schiller, then Deputy Division Chief in the IMF's Fiscal Affairs Department, has recommended specific sets of measures – liberalising trade systems, decontrolling prices, broadening the scope of marketisation – that are intended both to improve the quality of governance but also fight corruption. And Schiller claims that such approaches have successfully 'helped curtail that fertile ground for rent-seeking'.[70] Furthermore, in 1994 Vito Tanzi openly claimed that opportunities for corruption increase with a larger role for the state in the economy and in 1998 he developed this further by adding that government regulations per se and the public provision of goods and services at below market prices in particular prompt corruption.[71] When many of those active and influential within the IMF develop remedies from the philosophical and ideological starting points of the public choice school then it is not surprising that the policy advice that the organisation gives is unlikely to actually lead – in a sustained and systematic ways – to reductions in corruption levels.

The World Bank has been accused of falling into a similar trap although for many years the bank expressly avoided talking about, or analysing, corruption.[72] It did this on account of its Articles of Agreement forbidding it from engaging in a nation-state's domestic political affairs, and corruption was, quite rightly, seen as being a phenomenon with clear political attributes. Over the course of the 1990s, however, the bank carefully redefined its role, moving to understand corruption as both an economic and social issue rather than an overtly political one. By doing this it managed to increase the profile of anti-corruption work within the organisation – as is evidenced both by James Wolfensohn's call to attack corruption's cancerous qualities and the publication of a policy paper where it announced its intention to provide a 'systematic framework for addressing corruption as a development issue' – while still attempting to remain above the political fray.[73] By the 2000s even the World Bank itself realised that the attempt to claim that its reorientation towards fighting corruption while still remaining above politics was a pretence, and although the Bank still refrains from talking up its political role, there is now much more of a tacit awareness that the Bank does indeed inevitably make policy decisions that can have political consequences.

The Bank's change in approach involved a fundamental reassessment of the role of state institutions in facilitating market-led reforms. A new emphasis on 'governance, democratisation and institution-building' saw the Bank explicitly link 'arguments for economic liberalisation with those for the transformation of political systems'.[74] For some this was another clever way for a key pillar of the Washington Consensus to pursue its liberalising agenda in another form; the Bank was seen to be using the fight against corruption as another tool with which to push through (neo-liberal) structural reforms.[75] It appeared to see counteracting corruption as being essentially a technical issue that could be solved with particular types of (essentially more liberal) economic policy coupled with careful institutional reform.[76] Indeed, Heather Marquette, in arguably the most authoritative account of the World Bank's anti-corruption agenda thus far, claims that the considerable amount of research that World Bank experts have done as well as the Bank's practical efforts 'assume away the negative links between economic and political liberalisation and corruption' preferring instead to focus 'on only side of the debate'.[77]

One size doesn't fit all

A number of lessons can be drawn from the rise in the number of anti-corruption activities in recent years. Firstly, the advocacy and awareness-raising functions of groups such as Transparency International has ensured that corruption is now a policy challenge that is taken very seriously. Indeed, the development of a billion dollar anti-corruption industry has, given the ever-growing number of people who appear to live from it, left some with a rather nasty taste in the mouth. However, the fact that many people and many organisations are now involved in thinking about, and actively trying to fight, corruption should not detract from the seriousness with which they approach their work. Claims that the industry is too self-serving are subsequently almost certainly over-cooked.

The bigger issue for those interested in fighting corruption is a much simpler, and yet at the same time more challenging, one. Despite the development of numerous conventions, strategy papers, statements of intent, implementation mechanisms and monitoring schemes, levels of corruption do not appear to have systematically gone down. One doesn't have to be an enthusiast for TI's Corruption Perceptions Index to see that. Given the (financial and physical) investment put in, and indeed the ideological claims made, this is worrying. Part (although only part) of the explanation for this is that much of the mainstream academic discourse remains tied to remedies that fit well with a preordained scepticism about the ability of government to deliver efficient and effective services but does not fit with the complex political challenges faced by actors on the ground. The proposals that international organisations, and particularly the IMF and World Bank, developed through the 1990s and early 2000s largely bought in to public choice understandings of why corruption occurs, leading many programmes to be based 'simply on folk remedies or one-size-fits-all approaches that offer little chance of success'.[78] Whilst the prescriptions of these institutions are in many ways rather more nuanced than some of their popular caricatures, the empirical evidence suggesting that they have effectively tackled corrupt practices is thin at best. The notion that tackling corruption is in essence a technological challenge that can be met by effective implementation of liberalisation agendas subsequently needs re-thinking. And, as Chapter 2 will illustrate, through the 2000s some of this re-thinking did, and still is, indeed taking place.

One of the key lessons that needs to be learnt from the rapid rise of the anti-corruption industry is that context matters. International organisations and the academic analysts who provide their theoretical ammunition certainly pay lip service to this, but the practical remedies that these organisations have proposed have at times been disappointing. Only very recently have some of the prominent anti-corruption actors admitted – and even then often behind closed doors – that generalised programmes of (socio-economic, institutional and political) reforms have not provided solutions to what are in reality complex, place-specific and inherently political problems. One of the more promising avenues of research that looks to make good on the deficits analysed here involves the notion of 'quality of governance'. For some, governance remains a buzz word with little substance to it, but recent developments in understanding not just what the concept means but also 'how good' (or bad) a state's governance regime happens to be may well be useful in developing more fruitful approaches to tackling corruption. It is to these that Chapter 2 turns.

2
Governance Regimes and the Fight against Corruption

Introduction

The fight against corruption has, as Chapter 1 illustrated, moved on considerably since the late 1990s and early 2000s. The notion of countries fighting corruption by implementing sets of reforms linked explicitly to ideas of lean government and economic liberalisation is now decidedly passé. On the contrary, there is a widespread consensus that context needs to shape the anti-corruption reform agenda and that one-size-fits all approaches are unlikely to prove successful. The renewed emphasis on nuance has subsequently gone hand in hand with the rise of another agenda – that of improving a state's quality of governance.[1]

Notions of encouraging 'good governance' are clearly not new, but from the late 1990s onwards ever more interest has been shown in developing policies that sought to support it. Whilst a number of the key organisations that now actively promote ideas of good governance show a distinct sympathy towards government playing a limited role in shaping economic and social life, the logic of this approach does not by definition point in that direction. Indeed, governance ideas are now being used by a wide variety of organisations and authors 'of very different ideological persuasions' for 'a number of different and contradictory ends'.[2] For all their different usages, ideas of good governance none the less stress that understanding the quality of a country's governance – issues of how this is defined (let alone measured) not withstanding – is vital in pinpointing both what needs to be done to tackle corruption and also how one might best go about doing it. Whilst this approach is certainly not without its problems, it can none the less be used as a base from which to shape further research questions – and that is what the latter part of this chapter tries to do.

Good governance rather than lean government

The concept of governance (good, lean or otherwise) was not, of course, invented in the 1990s and the notion has been discussed in one way or another ever since governments began to exist. One of the first arenas where the concept made a noticeable return to prominence was in the development studies community where through the 1990s 'getting governance right' became both 'a means of achieving development and also a development objective in itself'.[3] In due course, those donating aid also began to link their benevolence directly or indirectly to issues of governance quality – a marked change to prevailing attitudes up until the late 1980s when the term governance was only heard very infrequently in development discourse.[4] And this in spite of the fact that the World Bank has actually used assessments of government performance – without explicitly linking this to broader ideas of 'governance' – to help it allocate resources since as early as the mid-1970s.[5]

There has subsequently been 'a veritable explosion of interest' in issues of governance.[6] And this across a range of academic disciplines. This rise in popularity of the term governance has not, of course, made defining it any easier. Some organisations – no doubt wary of the slipperiness of the concept – adopt definitions that are so broad that they are effectively meaningless, incorporating as an aspect 'good governance' more or less everything that is seen as being a progressive, productive force in society. Others, meanwhile, prefer narrower definitions, largely as they (understandably, perhaps) fit their particular interests. The World Bank, for example, claims that governance is the 'the exercise of political authority and the use of institutional resources to manage society's problems and affairs' whilst the UNDP uses very similar language in claiming that governance is 'the exercise of economic, political and administrative authority to manage a country's affairs at all levels'.[7] Over time the World Bank has actually produced a variety of definitions, some of which are narrow and relatively specific, others less so; in its 1992 report on governance and development it claimed, for example, that governance is 'the manner in which power is exercised in the management of a country's economic and social resources' whilst in 1994 it defined *good* governance as being 'epitomised by predictable, open and enlightened policy-making'.[8] By 2007 it was claiming that governance was 'the manner in which public officials and institutions acquire and exercise the authority to shape public policy and provide public goods and services'.[9]

Other international organisations generally use similar language; the OECD, for example, states that governance is simply 'the exercise of political, economic and administrative authority necessary to manage a nation's affairs', whilst UNESCAP (the United Nations Economic and Social Commission for Asia and the Pacific) defines governance as 'the process of decision-making and the process by which decisions are implemented (or not implemented)'.[10] The IMF, meanwhile, goes for the general approach, noting that governance 'encompasses all aspects of the way a country, corporation or other entity is governed'.[11] None of these definitions are necessarily wrong, but many of them are inevitably superficial, illustrating that defining governance to everyone's satisfaction is every bit as difficult as defining corruption. This has prompted some scholars to become sceptical both of the concept's en vogue-ness and subsequently of its use in actually shaping research agendas. Clark Gibson, a political scientist from UC San Diego, subsequently speaks for a not insignificant number when he claims that 'there is little analytic utility in using "governance" as a concept in the social sciences'.[12]

This many be a little too downbeat. Analyses of both governance and corruption certainly do suffer for having to encompass a wide range of definitions that are frequently developed for very specific purposes. Indeed, the nature of an organisation's remit – economic development, civil society support, aid delivery or whatever it may be – will inevitably impact on what it understands governance to be. However, there is, as there is with analysis of corruption, a reasonably wide consensus on the substance of what is in reality being discussed. Good governance, in other words, involves 'capable states' exercising clearly defined sets of functions 'operating under the rule of law'.[13] In essence governance subsequently refers to 'the traditions and institutions by which authority is exercised' and this will inevitably include 'the process by which governments are selected, monitored and replaced' as well as their ability to formulate and implement policy whilst securing 'the respect of citizens and the state for the institutions' that govern interactions between them.[14]

Much of the discussions in World Bank working papers and IMF think pieces subsequently state what is no doubt believed to be the obvious. States that are 'well governed' will have a greater chance of tackling corruption (and a range of other ills that have been inflicted on society). No one, in other words, is going to make a case for 'bad governance'. No one is going to deny that developing the rule of law and encouraging greater system legitimacy is anything other than a 'good thing' either. But, as with much of the thinking of those within these organisations on tackling corruption, the problems really lie in the detail of the assumptions that they make.

In terms of the implications of their (good) governance agendas, the pointers are certainly clear. For many in the organisations of international finance, 'work on good governance implies a one-best-way model of effective government'.[15] There is often precious little recognition that efficient, effective and legitimate (i.e. what most people would understand as 'good') governance regimes can often take on a variety of quite different appearances. In other words, the use of the term 'good governance' frequently still implies, in the words of Andersson and Heywood, a focus on 'improving political accountability, strengthening civil society, promoting competition via markets and the private sector, imposing institutional restraints on power and reforming public sector management'.[16] There remains a stress on the importance of incentive structures shaping behaviour and subsequently of minimising the opportunities to act in a corrupt fashion. The need to increase the costs of being caught goes hand in hand with this. Whilst 'making it harder to get away with it' clearly makes sense, there is a real danger of adopting a rather 'reductionist economism' that sees human beings behaving as they do simply as they are responding to complex sets of incentive structures.[17] 'Corruption control' according to Mlada Bukovansky 'thus becomes a technical matter of effectively manipulating incentive structures'.[18] The assumption in much of the literature therefore remains that if you 'fix the incentives' then you will solve the problem as getting these opportunity structures

– involving legal systems, institutions of government, the role of the media and so on – right will by definition improve governance and reduce levels of corruption.[19] Corruption and governance are subsequently seen more or less simply as 'institutional design problem[s]'.[20]

And yet – as many scholars have been quick to point out – tinkering with long-held and deeply engrained structures in the name of improving efficiency or effectiveness can regularly prompt grassroots confusion and dissatisfaction that can lead to precisely the opposite from happening. There is also a classic collective action problem at play here; constructing the broad, efficient and effective institutional framework that would be necessary to effectively shape such opportunity structures is – at best – extremely difficult, as the many societies that need such things most will be dominated by corrupt actors. And, it clearly is not in these actors' interest to help create any such institutional framework.[21] The advice that many international organisations subsequently give in trying to help countries develop structures of good governance (and with it to tackle corruption) assumes that they have the capacity to actually carry such things through. However, even if superficial improvements are made, the path dependent nature of highly corrupt societies is likely to prompt a form of 'self-correction' unless changes are deeply rooted and genuinely internalised.[22] For that to happen, more has to change than simply adopting new incentive structures.

Indicators of governance

What does the apparent failure of these quite specific notions of *good* governance mean for the aim of tackling corruption? More pressingly, does governance as a concept still have a meaningful role to play? The answer to the second question is certainly more positive than the answer to the first; notions of good governance may have been hijacked by those with a particular ideological agenda, but ideas concerning the *quality* of governance certainly still have plenty to offer. The question now is no longer really one of applying sets of more or less technocratic solutions, it is how does one develop nuanced sets of possible remedies that 'fit' with local circumstances?

The problems inherent in the practical implementation of notions of 'good governance' have not, however, put off those attempting to quantify governance more generally. You do not have to be a supporter of the 'good governance' agenda to believe that creating approximate indicators, if carefully and skilfully constructed, of *governance quality* should be possible. It would be very naïve to believe that any one set of indicators could provide definitive answers, but if indicators are used in the way that their name suggests – i.e. to *indicate* rather than to speak absolute truths – then they can be very useful indeed in illustrating deficiencies across all (i.e. rich, poor, developed, not-so-developed) states.

With this in mind, there are now as many indices of the quality of (various aspects of) governance as there are of the scope and extent of corruption. On the one hand, this should not really come as too much of a surprise. Developing political indicators is not a new enterprise, and organisations such as Freedom House have, for example, been collecting data in order to measure the extent of civil liberties and political rights since the early 1970s.[23] In recent times there has, however, been an exponential rise in the number of indices proclaiming explicitly to measure aspects of governance. Pippa Norris has noted 'literally dozens' whilst Christiane Arndt and Charles Oman go as far as claiming that there are now 'hundreds' of these indices, some of which have enjoyed (considerable) success, both in the sense of fulfilling the aims they set themselves and also in influencing policy-makers, whilst others are barely noticed outside the institutions that helped create them.[24] Gauging the quality of things as wide and varied as civic engagement, social capital, human rights, women's empowerment and of course good governance is now subsequently a more developed exercise than ever.[25]

As with attempts to measure corruption, many of the indicators of governance quality base their governance scores on the perceptions of country experts, of those with direct experience in the field and also increasingly of households. Many of the methodological criticisms that can be made of Transparency International (and others) in terms of their attempts to measure corruption can – and have been – subsequently levelled at those who try to quantify the quality of governance.[26] Some claim that these indicators may prove to be unreliable as they can rely on relatively small numbers of national 'experts' for the bulk of their data, whilst Christiane Arndt and Charles Oman make the further claim that governance indicators in general, and the WGI indicators (see below) in particular, have a tendency to stress the opinions of business leaders over those of other stakeholders.[27] There have also been a series of criticisms about governance indicators either under-estimating, or simply not being transparent about, the scope and extent of the variations in country coverage across the different indices.[28] As Edward Glaser and colleagues note, countries with better economic fortunes may enjoy an unintended bias in evaluations over those with greater economic difficulties, although a number of prominent authors in the field produce strong evidence refuting this.[29] Finally, there is also the inevitable fixation on the minutiae of methodological issues that seem to fascinate some commentators.[30] All that not withstanding 'these measures provide some of the best available gauges of good governance' and they can – with suitable caution – offer valuable pointers for policy-makers.[31]

World Governance Indicators

Of all the various attempts to measure and analyse quality of governance in different states around the world, the most well-known, the most ambitious and arguably the most impressive are the 'World Governance Indicators' (WGI). The WGI have long been overseen by Daniel Kaufmann, Aart Kraay and their colleagues at the World Bank Institute.[32] First published in 1996, they are composite indices that seek to measure perceived levels of governance quality across six specific dimensions. The dimensions are:[33]

1. *Voice and Accountability* – This captures perceptions of the extent to which a country's citizens are able to participate in selecting the government, how free they are to express their own feelings and attitudes in public, to what extent freedom of association is permitted and finally how free and open the media is.
2. *Political Stability and Absence of Violence/Terrorism* – This dimensions aims to capture perceptions of the likelihood that a government will be destabilised or overthrown by unconstitutional or violent means. This includes both politically-motivated violence and terrorism.
3. *Government Effectiveness* – This captures perceptions of the quality of public services, the quality of the civil service and how independent it is perceived to be from political pressures. It also

captures perceptions of the quality of policy formulation and implementation, as well as the credibility of the government's commitment to carrying such policies through.

4. *Regulatory Quality* – This dimension captures perceptions of the ability (as opposed to the quality – see point 3) of the government to formulate and implement sound policies and to develop regulations that permit and promote private sector development.

5. *Rule of Law* – This captures perceptions of the extent to which agents have confidence in, and abide by, the rules that govern society. In particular, this dimension looks at the quality of contract enforcement, property rights, the police, and the courts, as well as the likelihood of being affected by either crime and/or violence.

6. *Control of Corruption* – The final dimension captures perceptions of the extent to which public power is exercised for private gain, including both petty and grand forms of corruption, as well as 'capture' of the state by elites and private interests.

The WGI now use data on 212 countries and territories, based on 35 data sources from 33 different organisations. The data reflects the perceptions of a wide array of 'informed stakeholders', whether they are country experts, households, representatives from NGOs or members of the business community. Kaufmann et al. are quick to recognise the limitations of the WGI as perception based indicators, but they defend their use for three specific reasons. Firstly, they argue that perceptions matter 'as agents base their actions on perceptions, impressions and views'. If, in other words, people believe something to be true then it will by definition affect their behaviour. Secondly, so-called 'objective indicators' claim to take subjective influences out of the equation, but in reality there are very few – if indeed any – genuinely objective indicators available. In reality, so the authors claim, there are few alternatives to using perceptions based data. Finally, even when 'objective' indicators may be readily available – they give the example of laws, rules and regulations – how they are implemented can often be substantially different from how they *should* be implemented.[34] The WGI subsequently uses aggregate indicators to organise a large and diverse amount of data and they report not only the generalised trends but also the disaggregated scores for the vast majority of the individual indicators. Indeed, these can – with but a few minor exceptions – all be downloaded from the WGI's impressive website.[35]

Kaufmann and colleagues are very keen to stress that their measures are also explicit in highlighting the statistical margins of error associated with each and every estimate; these are, so they claim, part and parcel of the measurement process and including them is a recognition of the 'unavoidable uncertainty' that goes hand in hand with the process of measuring any abstract concept.[36] They are not slow in pointing the finger at other attempts to measure governance that choose not to be so revealing.[37] Despite the fact that these margins of error are inherent in all indicators of governance, Kaufmann et al. none the less claim that the margins of error in the WGI have declined over time and that the data 'do not reveal statistically (or likely practically) significant differences in governance'.[38] They believe, in other words, that their indicators are both reliable and revealing.

Naturally, this has not rendered them above criticism, and a significant number of authors have pointed out what they argue are both methodological and philosophical problems with Kaufmann et al's. approach.[39] Indeed, Kaufmann and colleagues have not shirked the challenge of responding to their critics.[40] There is no need to analyse all of the claims and counter claims made here, but the general thrust of the criticisms can be summarised in four points.

Firstly, as with all governance indicators (indeed *all* such indicators across all fields), there have been criticisms of the way that the scores in the indicators are calculated. Serious though these issues are, such debates can often descend into arguments about the minutiae of model creation. It is easy, in other words, to pick holes in most such approaches if one is that way inclined. In terms of the WGI, the debate tends either to centre round discrepancies between what the indicators purport to measure and what they actually do measure (assuming that they do indeed measure something), as well as problems that are inherent in correlating data from different sources. This includes issues of how independent the data sources are from one another.[41]

Kaufmann et al. are certainly prepared to admit that the indicators they have developed are not the finished article and whilst always robust in defending them they do recognise that there can be, on occasion, a number of ways of skinning the proverbial cat.

For example, they do acknowledge – as anyone undertaking such an enterprise would (or at least should) – that margins of error exist and need to be noted, but they are equally as robust in dismissing accusations that their indicators are not reliable enough as 'either ... entirely lacking in empirical support' or even when there is some empirical evidence supporting these criticisms 'the effects are so small as to be practically irrelevant'.[42] They give a prescient example in response to criticisms by Stephen Knack concerning the fact that the average indicators are scaled to give them a mean of zero.[43] In practice, this means that the WGI look to have zero as an average with countries registering scores either above or below that score. Over time, however, the number of countries included in the WGI has increased, hence a country may theoretically have registered the same score across time but will actually see its performance affected without having done anything at all to warrant such a change. Kaufmann et al. enthusiastically take up this point by illustrating that in 1996 they possessed data on 152 countries in terms of controlling corruption. By 2005 they had data for 204 countries. Over time, the averages will inevitably have changed simply as a result of more countries coming on board. However, Kaufmann et al. ran a variety of tests on their data to try and discern the impact of this – again, they plausibly argue that although the criticisms are technically correct, the net effect on the data as a whole is nothing more than negligible.[44]

Secondly, and linked with the first point, Arndt and Oman in particular have pointed out that individual country scores are likely to be computed over time using slightly different data sets (i.e. as new data sources come on stream and some are no longer collected) whilst data sources are likely to vary across countries. This leads Arndt and Oman to claim that the 'indicators do not allow for a reliable comparison of governance over time'.[45] Indeed, it is plausible – although not particularly likely – that some countries' scores will be computed from a completely different set of data (i.e. with no overlapping sources at all) to that of other countries. These observations are – in the most basic sense – plainly valid, but Kaufmann et al. are quick to point out that they have made adjustments to the mean of the aggregate governance indicators to 'recognise this changing sample composition'. In their words 'while technically this point is correct, practically it turns out not to matter much'.[46] Plus, of course, if one were only to limit oneself to comparing countries with identical sets of data then conducting comparative research would become very much more difficult.

Thirdly, they take on the much discussed issue of whose opinions are actually being represented. Knack in particular claims that the opinions of businessmen are likely to feature too prominently in the WGI while Arndt and Oman claim both that there is a 'sample bias in favour of business-oriented perceptions' and that the opinions of everyday people 'carry practically no weight'.[47] Again, Kaufmann et al. dispute this, and the data they provide appears convincing. In 2005, for example, there were indeed four cross country surveys of firms as well as seven from commercial ratings agencies (which are very likely to concentrate on speaking to those in the business community). However, there were also three surveys of individuals as well as six sets of data that were produced by governments and multilateral organisations. Finally, another 11 sources were produced by non-governmental organisations such as Reporters without Borders and Freedom House. They therefore bluntly claim that it is 'simply incorrect to dismiss our indicators as reflecting solely – or even primarily – the narrow interests of the business elite'. Furthermore, they finish this particular rebuttal by stressing that 'it is implausible that the preferences of business people' about the quality of governance in their particular state will 'differ so dramatically from those of other types of respondents' anyway.[48]

Finally, Knack, Arndt and Oman and Thomas all explicitly accuse the WGI authors of failing to publish all of the data on which they calculate their composite scores. Knack claims that some of the sources are only available to paying customers whilst others are not available at all.[49] Arndt and Oman come up with a range of what they claim are transparency problems, ranging from the shear complexity and at times opacity that is inherent in some of the composite indicators to the absence of a 'list of criteria that each source uses to determine its country rankings'.[50] Thomas even goes as far as claiming that this means that results obtained via all governance indicators (WGI included) 'are uninterpretable and should not survive peer review' – a serious claim for any social scientist to make of others' work.[51] Unsurprisingly, these accusations receive short thrift. Kaufmann et al. do acknowledge that they are unable – for reasons of confidentiality requested by the organisation – to fully publish data from the 'Country Policy and Institutional Assessment' (CPIA), but that caveat aside everything else is available via the WGI's website.[52] Admittedly, some of it is only available on a commercial basis, but available it none the less is. For this reason difficult and no doubt cumbersome though it would be to replicate in its entirety what the WGI authors do, it is possible to see how they have come to the conclusions that they have.

Using the World Governance Indicators

Given that the WGI data appears to be both well constructed and widely accepted as useful, it offers a sufficiently rigorous base from which to conduct more detailed research. Importantly, in terms of substantive findings, the data certainly does not lead one to conclude that there is a right and proper way of organising the institutions of a given state. It may well be the case that the Nordic countries come out consistently well across all indicators (as does New Zealand, for that matter), and that they have managed to maintain these high quality of governance levels over significant periods of time. Yet governments – rich and poor – across all parts of the globe face 'serious challenges' on account of what Kaufmann terms 'sub-par governance'.[53] Indeed, Kaufmann illustrates that if one takes the G20 countries as a point of reference, then the average of their respective scores in 2010 in terms of 'rule of law' is lower than 75 countries that are not G20 members. Furthermore, if one did the same calculation for the 'voice and accountability' indicator then 86 countries would rank above the G20 average. Conversely, a whole host of countries have better governance scores across a number of indicators than do Italy and Greece. While some countries have shown noticeable improvements across a number of dimensions (some from very low previous levels, others not so) there is also plenty of evidence that governance quality can slip.[54] In short, it is just the type of data that should offer useful pointers for seeking to help the interested observer understand the governance challenges that each and every country faces.

The detailed, data-heavy statistical analysis provided by scholars linked to the WGI project subsequently prompts, perhaps curiously, the authors to make pretty similar claims to those who adopt much more interpretist approaches to analysing when and why corruption occurs (and even what it actually is). 'Policy-makers' claims Anwar Shah from the World Bank, for example, need to 'understand the local circumstances that encourage or permit public and private actors to be corrupt', whilst the anthropologist Elizabeth Harrison has stressed the importance of 'understanding the social character-istics which influence corruption'.[55] In essence, they are both calling for a greater understanding of the institutional – understood in its broadest sense – specifics of each individual setting before mapping out anti-corruption strategies.

Scholars who understand the importance of governance quality have subsequently begun to develop menus listing possible options for reform rather than simply 'to-do lists'. Huther and Shah, for example, say that the most appropriate items from these menus will differ considerably and will be dependent on the quality of gover-nance that a state already exhibits. Particular types of reform could well (they are careful not to claim that they 'will') actually have neg-ative effects on governance quality if employed in the wrong way and/or at the wrong time.[56] Shah and Schacter take this further by putting states that score well across most indicators in a broadly defined 'good quality' category. This category generally fits states where the 'governance fundamentals' are reasonably sound and although corruption exists it tends to be something of a second order issue.[57] Given that, particular sets of anti-corruption mech-anisms and processes are seen as being most likely as having an impact. States with clear divisions of power and a culture of transparency and accountability may want to consider empowering independent, powerful anti-corruption agencies to look at alleged misdemeanours.[58] Such agencies, they claim, are much more likely to have an impact where the rule of law is well-respected and where their work will not be politically compromised. It is here that 'catch-ing the big fish' is both feasible and desirable, sending out the message that corrupt practices will no longer be tolerated. Where the quality of governance is good there may well be a case for strengthening the financial accountability of political parties and other political actors, opening up to closer political scrutiny tradi-tionally controversial issues such as party funding and the role of the private sector in funding political activities. Only in states where there is faith in, and trust of, independent actors being allowed to fulfil such oversight remits will they – the new laws, or the new institutions overseeing political practice – be able to genuinely do their work.

States that do not do quite so well – or that perform well in some areas but poorly in others – are likely to need to look at different parts of the anti-corruption menu. These states, states that 'assume a modicum of governance capacity' and are subsequently 'fair' in governance terms, are likely to need to sharpen up processes of parliamentary oversight, to look to try and make civil servants more directly accountable for their decisions, to improve the right of the media to investigate allegedly corrupt acts, to simplify administrative procedures and generally to reduce the amount of discretion available to public servants.[59] This is not by definition a call to shrink the state, but it is a call to try and increase both the transparency and accountability of the state's affairs.

Table 2.1   Quality of governance and anti-corruption mechanisms[60]

Levels of Corruption	Quality of Governance	Hypothesised Anti-Corruption Methods
High	Poor	Establish rule of law; strengthen institutions of participation and accountability; establish citizens' charter; introduce judicial independence; implement economic policy reforms.
Fair	Fair	Decentralise and reform economic policies, increase parliamentary oversight and increase efficiency and effectiveness of public management.
Low	Good	Establish anti-corruption agencies; strengthen financial accountability; raise public and official awareness; encourage anti-bribery pledges; conduct high-profile prosecutions.

Finally, states that have 'poor' governance regimes are likely to need to concentrate on an altogether different set of issues and challenges. Here, the answer to alleviating corruption may well lie 'in taking an indirect approach and starting with the root causes' of poor governance.[61] This approach is, of course, not simply aimed at tackling corruption, but also at fighting a wide range of other governance problems. In practice, this is likely to involve small steps geared towards improving the most basic elements of the state's governance regime. This makes sense as overt campaigns to tackle corruption have as much chance of backfiring as they do of being successful. Indeed, such campaigns will frequently become tools of those in power and/or will simply be warm words that prompt little in the way of substantive change. In these circumstances the rule of law itself may well need strengthening and citizen participation in political processes – however small this participation may be at first – should be encouraged. Many of the reforms in this category, outlined in Table 2.1, are both fundamental in nature and particularly difficult to implement; it is here that we come across the collective action problem (i.e. fundamental reform requires the buy in of those with most to lose) in its starkest forms, and ways forward will also certainly need to be small in scale, very focused on what is achievable in the national context and necessarily long-term in nature.

Reforms in practice

The framework outlined above is necessarily broad, and clearly needs adapting to each and every set of specific circumstances. The specific parts of it also need to be tested against what has actually happened in practice. To an extent, this has taken place already – a not inconsiderable number of studies exist both on the anti-corruption efforts in specific countries, but also on the merits or otherwise of particular anti-corruption initiatives. A number of studies have analysed the effectiveness of anti-corruption agencies, for example, whilst there has also been considerable effort put in to testing to what extent raising the wages of civil servants acts as a successful antidote to corruption (the consensus on this being 'very little', hence it does not merit a place in the above framework).[62] There have also been a significant number of studies on the role of the media, the importance of citizen participation, bureaucratic cultures, the effect of reducing the size of the public sector and whether increasing financial accountability really does reduce corruption levels.[63]

In terms of country specific analyses of both corruption and anti-corruption we find, again, that there is no lack of (often decidedly descriptive) analyses of individual countries or of one specific sector or type of anti-corruption mechanism.[64] Both of these types of

analysis are no doubt useful, but they do not really offer the com-
paritivist much to work with. There is effectively nothing comparing and contrasting the anti-corruption approaches of countries
across the spectrum of governance regimes outlined above. This is
precisely what the chapters in the rest of this book aim to do.

The WGI data – imperfect though it naturally is – offers the perfect
tool for shaping research design in this area, and it is with that in
mind that the paired comparisons chosen in Chapters 3, 4 and 5
have been selected. There would be little point in picking states
with similar governance snapshots in 2011, hence the empirical
sections are based on the snapshots as they were in 1999, 2000 and
2001. Each of the following chapters subsequently begins both with
a description of the respective governance regimes of each state in
this period before outlining the anti-corruption approaches – both
in theory and in practice – that have been implemented since then.
This allows us to track the reasons for the respective successes and
failures over a sustained period of time, noting lessons to be drawn
along the way.

In terms of states with 'poor' quality governance snapshots,
Chapter 3 puts the cases of Bangladesh and Kenya under the analytical
microscope. Their less than glowing governance records (see Chapter 3)
were reflected in Transparency International's Corruption Perception
Index (CPI). In 2001 Bangladesh registered a meagre 0.9 whilst
Kenya was on an uninspiring 2.0. However, by 2011 Bangladesh had
improved its rating to 2.7 whereas Kenya's score had hardly moved
(2.2). As Chapter 1 illustrated, the CPI is meant only to give 'ball
park' indications (i.e. one should not emphasise small differences
in scores too much), but 'something' in Bangladesh clearly appeared
to be working whereas that did not appear to be the case in Kenya.
Much more importantly for our purposes, we can see whether
Bangladesh had implemented – and was benefiting from – some of
the anti-corruption mechanisms highlighted in Table 2.1, namely
from doing one or a number of the following; reducing the size
of the public sector, granting the media and judiciary more independence, increasing citizen participation in political and civic
life and/or strengthening the rule of law. These moves, according
to Huther and Shah at least, theoretically reduce potential for corruption by moving decision-making into the open and away from
the hands of corrupt public servants whilst assisting interested

parties (citizens, the media, other institutions) who seek to detect corrupt practices.[65]

In Chapter 4 exactly the same approach is adopted in an analysis of the anti-corruption initiatives in South Korea and Poland, both of which could, at the end of the 20th century, be categorised as 'fair' in terms of the quality of their governance. Both states appear to have made progress in terms of their CPI scores; in 2001 South Korea registered 4.2 whereas Poland got 4.1. By 2011 both had made considerable improvements, South Korea moving up to 5.4 and Poland to 5.5. Again, the CPI numbers should not be taken as hard evidence, but they do indicate that something has improved noticeably in both states. Chapter 4 analyses to what extent these CPI scores correspond with reality on the ground by analysing which of the following (if indeed any at all) have been implemented and have correspondingly affected corrupt practices; an increased emphasis on a merit based civil service, more parliamentary oversight, strengthening of media and judicial independence, the use of anti-corruption commissions, and a reduction in public sector size. As with the first paired comparison, we also investigate whether and how other policies have impacted on corruption.[66]

In terms of the final substantive chapter (analysing 'good' governance categories), the analysis moves to the UK and Germany. In 2001 the UK found itself scoring 8.3 in the CPI whereas Germany registered a score of 7.4. By 2011, these roles had again been reversed, the UK slipping 0.5 points (to 7.8), whereas Germany had improved by 0.6 points (to 8.0). Here, the analysis takes a broad view, but a particular emphasis is placed on whether explicit anti-corruption laws and programmes have had an impact, high-profile convictions have been secured and whether accountability processes have been strengthened. Such reforms should, in theory at least, increase accountability and processes of integrity management as public servants become (more) aware that their principals are paying greater attention to their work, whilst putting high profile miscreants on trial should not only raise awareness but also send out clear messages that everyone is equal in front of the law. Lessons for anti-corruption strategists elsewhere will then be drawn in the conclusion.

3
Bangladesh and Kenya: Tough Talk, Small Steps, Ineffectual Outcomes

Introduction

Tackling corruption in states with low quality governance regimes is, to put it mildly, challenging. This chapter illustrates this by looking at two cases – Bangladesh and Kenya – that, whilst in many ways are very different, have faced broadly similar sets of governance dilemmas. Indeed, there are a number of good reasons to compare and contrast their respective fortunes. First and foremost, both countries have serious, long-standing and deeply embedded corruption problems. The challenges they face are therefore similarly large. Both countries have also experienced periods of authoritarian rule, but both are now (imperfect) multi-party democracies. Both remain predominantly rural, have similar per capita income and economic structures and are former British colonies.[1] There are therefore good reasons for comparing and contrasting their performances in terms of tackling corruption.

The WGI data gives us some indication of the nature of the challenges that these countries face, as both Tables 3.1 and 3.2 illustrate. The data covers the period from 1996–2002 and records how the respective countries performed across each of the six WGI indicators. The percentile rank illustrates how both Bangladesh and Kenya faired in comparison with other countries. The next column reveals the governance score per indicator per year. A score of zero would indicate a position where half of the other countries performed better on average for that indicator, whilst half performed worse, with scores of –2.5 and +2.5 being the respective (bad and good) ends of the spectrum. Importantly, the standard errors are also included here, indicating how robust the data is.

As is to be expected, the quality of governance during this period varied considerably across both time and indicator-type, and there is evidence both of improvement and decline in Bangladesh and Kenya. Neither country, however, managed at any time during this period and for any specific indicator to register a score that would have placed them in the top half in terms of governance quality. The story is therefore one of very poor performance at worst (as was the case in Bangladesh in 2002 in terms of 'control of corruption') to below average performance at best (something that both countries registered at specific times and across a number of indicators).

The picture here is much as Kaufmann et al. would have predicted. Between 1996–2002 both countries exhibited better quality of governance than might have been expected in some areas, whilst performing poorly in others. As was noted in Chapter 2, the story of governance quality is one of nuance. Here, this was particularly evident in the area of 'voice and accountability' and also 'government effectiveness', where both countries performed reasonably (see Tables 3.1 and 3.2). In terms of 'voice and accountability', both are democracies – in the case of Bangladesh a 'chaotic and corrupt' democracy, whilst in Kenya democracy has often been plagued by 'coercion, co-optation, and the systematic manipulation of the electoral process' – but they are democracies nonetheless, so it should not be too surprising that citizens do have at least some opportunity to articulate their preferences.[2] This is certainly much truer in Bangladesh and Kenya than it is of authoritarian states such as China (with scores and similar standard errors between 1996–2002 of –1.29, –1.38, –1.27 and –1.57 respectively) or Saudi Arabia (–1.39, –1.52, –1.49 and –1.64), not to mention the worst performer during this period, North Korea (–1.95, –2.12, –2.14, –2.13). The two states under the microscope here subsequently perform better than a number of others.

In terms of 'government effectiveness', elites in both countries may well have manipulated the political process to suit their own ends, just as they have developed elaborate corrupt practices both to look after their friends and to preserve their own positions in power, but the governments have – for better or worse – also been able to

Table 3.1   The quality of governance in Bangladesh, 1996–2002

Governance Indicator	Sources	Year	Percentile Rank (0–100)	Governance Score (−2.5 – +2.5)	Standard Error
Voice and	8	2002	37.0	−0.45	0.17
Accountability	6	2000	39.4	−0.28	0.22
	5	1998	41.8	−0.26	0.23
	5	1996	46.6	−0.15	0.22
Political	5	2002	17.3	−1.07	0.29
Stability	4	2000	23.6	−0.74	0.33
	4	1998	29.8	−0.49	0.32
	4	1996	24.5	−0.65	0.36
Government	7	2002	26.8	−0.72	0.16
Effectiveness	6	2000	32.2	−0.56	0.17
	4	1998	39.0	−0.43	0.21
	3	1996	24.9	−0.73	0.25
Regulatory	8	2002	18.1	−1.01	0.21
Quality	7	2000	18.6	−0.87	0.24
	5	1998	17.6	−0.89	0.30
	4	1996	16.2	−1.05	0.32
Rule of Law	10	2002	22.0	−0.90	0.17
	9	2000	22.0	−0.90	0.16
	6	1998	19.6	−0.92	0.21
	5	1996	16.7	−0.96	0.22
Control of	6	2002	5.4	−1.18	0.17
Corruption	6	2000	12.7	−0.96	0.20
	4	1998	38.5	−0.44	0.21
	3	1996	27.3	−0.74	0.30

Source: http://info.worldbank.org/governance/wgi/sc_chart.asp# viewed on
28th December 2011

deliver some services more effectively than a significant number of other states. Again, the performance may well be 'below average' in terms of the world as a whole, but there are others who have been performing much worse.

Table 3.2 The quality of governance in Kenya, 1996–2002

Governance Indicator	Sources	Year	Percentile Rank (0–100)	Governance Score (–2.5 – +2.5)	Standard Error
Voice and	9	2002	27.4	–0.71	0.17
Accountability	6	2000	25.5	–0.78	0.21
	5	1998	21.6	–0.88	0.23
	5	1996	32.7	–0.56	0.22
Political	4	2002	15.4	–1.27	0.31
Stability	4	2000	15.9	–1.11	0.33
	4	1998	17.3	–0.92	0.32
	4	1996	20.2	–0.78	0.36
Government	7	2002	27.3	–0.70	0.17
Effectiveness	5	2000	35.1	–0.54	0.21
	5	1998	34.1	–0.49	0.20
	3	1996	43.4	–0.34	0.25
Regulatory	8	2002	45.1	–0.20	0.21
Quality	6	2000	37.3	–0.30	0.24
	6	1998	35.3	–0.34	0.27
	4	1996	36.3	–0.37	0.32
Rule of Law	9	2002	24.4	–0.85	0.18
	7	2000	23.4	–0.89	0.17
	7	1998	14.4	–1.10	0.20
	5	1996	16.3	–0.98	0.22
Control of	6	2002	15.6	–0.99	0.19
Corruption	5	2000	14.6	–0.95	0.24
	5	1998	12.2	–1.03	0.20
	3	1996	15.1	–1.03	0.30

Source: http://info.worldbank.org/governance/wgi/sc_chart.asp# viewed on 28th December 2011

In terms of 'control of corruption', the data is particularly interesting.[3] The data in Tables 3.3. and 3.4 spans not just the period from 1996–2002, but has also been brought up to 2010. For Bangladesh, the data for 1996 and 1998 comes from only a small number of sources and the standard errors are higher than for all other years, but the indication is that the government was seen to be doing a below average but not abysmal job of controlling corruption. During the first half of the noughties, however, Bangladesh's performance – based on data from more sources with lower standard errors – slips

Table 3.3   Control of corruption, Bangladesh, 1996–2010

Country	Sources	Year	Percentile Rank (0–100)	Governance Score (–2.5 – +2.5)	Standard Error
Bangladesh	13	2010	16.30	–0.99	0.17
	12	2009	16.70	–1.00	0.17
	12	2008	14.60	–1.01	0.16
	12	2007	11.20	–1.04	0.17
	11	2006	3.90	–1.41	0.16
	9	2005	4.90	–1.42	0.18
	9	2004	2.40	–1.46	0.19
	7	2003	3.90	–1.34	0.18
	6	2002	5.40	–1.18	0.17
	6	2000	12.70	–0.96	0.20
	4	1998	38.50	–0.44	0.21
	3	1996	27.30	–0.74	0.30

Source: WGI data, accessed 28th December 2011

Table 3.4   Control of corruption, Kenya, 1996–2010

Country	Sources	Year	Percentile Rank (0–100)	Governance Score (–2.5 – +2.5)	Standard Error
Kenya	14	2010	18.7	–0.91	0.16
	14	2009	13.4	–1.05	0.16
	14	2008	13.6	–1.01	0.15
	13	2007	17.5	–0.92	0.16
	14	2006	20.0	–0.86	0.15
	14	2005	17.1	–0.98	0.17
	10	2004	20.5	–0.86	0.17
	9	2003	22.4	–0.81	0.19
	6	2002	15.6	–0.99	0.19
	5	2000	14.6	–0.95	0.24
	5	1998	12.2	–1.03	0.20
	3	1996	15.1	–1.03	0.30

Source: WGI data, accessed 28th December 2011

badly, and the country consistently finds itself in the worst percentile. Only post-2007 does this appear (again with more data to work with and fractionally lower standard errors than before) to improve, although the governance scores remain around the −1.0 mark, indicating that corruption is a serious problem.

The picture for Kenya is more consistent than is the case for Bangladesh, but it is only marginally more encouraging. Never between 1996–2010 did Kenya find itself in the bottom 10 per cent of states, but never did it really threaten to control corruption enough so as to move out of the 10th–25th percentile. Kenya's scores hover around the −1.0 point, occasionally improving (2003 and 2004) but also occasionally slipping below that figure (1996, 1998, 2008 and 2009). Scores based on more data sources that are accompanied by lower standard errors have little impact on Kenya's performance, indicating that the picture across the entire period is likely to be both reasonably accurate and reasonably stable.

Despite the fact that politicians in both Bangladesh and Kenya (see below) launched high profile anti-corruption drives, the data for both states illustrates that in order for corruption to be meaningfully tackled then the following, as was discussed on page 44 and in Table 2.1, would appear to be more appropriate:

- take steps to deepen and expand the rule of law and the importance of legal objectivity
- strengthen in whatever ways possible the institutions of, and processes that underpin, greater participation and accountability in public life
- develop and embed citizens' charters that pinpoint the rights, obligations, responsibilities and duties of the state vis-à-vis citizens (and vice-versa)
- introduce, or increase, the independence of the judiciary from the legislature and primarily the executive
- implement policy reforms that have transparency as a core principle, subsequently limiting the number and scope of situations where officials might exercise unaccountable discretionary powers.

Rather than simply list the anti-corruption initiatives that governments (and others) have sought to pursue, the rest of this chapter will analyse the key successes and failures evident in each state.

Again, this is not a list-making exercise, and the aim of the case study analysis here is to illustrate where progress was (and was not) made and, crucially, why that was the case.

Tackling corruption in Bangladesh

Bangladesh, as befits a country that occupied the last rank on TI's Corruption Perceptions Index from 2001 to 2005, has deeply engrained sets of corruption-related problems. Corruption has become 'a dominant component of its bureaucratic culture' and 'institutionalised in the public service'.[4] Despite nearly 40 years of on-off democracy, corruption remains 'pervasive and unabated'[5] as politics continues to be dominated by 'personalities and political cliques'.[6] Corruption, as Almas Zakiuddin succinctly puts it, 'reaches far, wide and deep' and spans 'the senior bureaucracy to the far-flung corners of the country', encompassing 'the apex of political activity to the minute activities of a rural community'.[7] In very few places can it be said that tackling corruption is as important as it is in Bangladesh.

Table 3.5   **Bangladesh's performance in Transparency International's Corruption Perceptions Index, 2001–2011**

Year	Score	Rank
2001	0.4	91 (out of 91)
2002	1.2	102 (out of 102)
2003	1.3	133 (out of 133)
2004	1.5	145 (joint last out of 146)
2005	1.7	158 (joint last out of 159)
2006	2.0	156 (out of 163)
2007	2.0	162 (out of 180)
2008	2.1	147 (out of 180)
2009	2.4	139 (out of 180)
2010	2.4	134 (out of 178)
2011	2.7	120 (out of 183)

Source: Transparency International's Website. Scores were not registered for Bangladesh before 2001

The factors that underpin Bangladesh's corruption problems are manifold, but in essence, and as Mohammed Mohabbat Khan has argued, they can be bundled together into four groups.[8] Firstly, should public servants be caught acting in what is legally understood as a corrupt fashion, then only in very few cases will they lose their jobs. Khan claims that incidences of imprisonment are equally as infrequent and, crucially, it is extremely rare indeed for officials to be required to return ill-gotten gains. Iftekharuzzaman concurs, noting that corruption 'affects almost everyone and is hardly ever punished'.[9] The costs of being caught are subsequently much lower than the rewards on offer to those who indulge themselves. Secondly, law enforcement officials themselves are particularly prone to be corrupt. The temptation is often to share the spoils rather than to deal with corrupt public servants in the ways that the law theoretically demands. Colin Knox illustrates this perfectly by claiming that in 2009 a mind-boggling 96.6 per cent of households that interacted with law enforcement agencies claimed to have experienced some form of corruption.[10]

Thirdly, there has been a tendency on the part of citizens not just to tolerate corruption but even to respect those who are seen as clever and savvy enough to use their office to look after themselves, their friends and their families. The fact that money is often made through dubious means can frequently be overlooked; on the contrary, public servants who play the game and manipulate rules to suit themselves are seen as being worthy both of emulation and admiration. Finally, in practical terms citizens are quick to realise – and who can blame them – that acting in a corrupt way (i.e. paying a bribe) is simply the easiest and most efficient way for them to get the service or outcome that they require. Corrupt means, in other words, are widely perceived to grease the wheels and to help ensure that preferred outcomes come quickly, efficiently and effectively.

Bangladeshi governments of all colours have not been slow to recognise these problems. Although Bangladesh gained formal independence in 1971, within five years the military had taken over and the generals ruled from 1976–1991. On its return to democratic government, Bangladeshi politics came to be dominated by the Bangladesh Nationalist Party (BNP) and the Awami League (AL). Both parties recognised the corruption problem, although both were quick to criticise the other as being the main cause of it and/or hindrance to tackling it. Over time, the relationship between the BNP and the AL – and particularly that of their respective leaders, Khaleda Zia and Sheikh Hasina – became completely dysfunctional and election losers regularly refused to accept their respective defeats. This led to a succession of parliamentary boycotts, general political instability, to regular strikes (or 'hartals') as well as worsening corruption. By January 2007 a state of emergency had been declared and a military-backed caretaker government had been put in place. This situation lasted nearly two years, and only came to an end when the theoretically technocratic administration called an election for late December 2008. This election was won handsomely by the opposition AL, campaigning on a platform that had anti-corruption very much at its core.[11]

Top down anti-corruption attempts

As indicated above, governments of all colours have claimed that they want to tackle corruption. This has led to a series of high-profile, top-down campaigns involving new legislation, the introduction of new institutions and indeed ultimately the high-profile arrests of politicians. Despite initial enthusiasm amongst much of the Bangladeshi population, the success of these attempts has been at best minimal.

The most extreme of these top-down anti-corruption measures came about in 2007–2008, when the military-backed caretaker government headed by Fakhruddin Ahmed, a former official at the World Bank, launched an anti-corruption crusade through 2007 and 2008. The concept of a caretaker government is firmly embedded in Bangladeshi political culture, with a temporary administration taking over for the period between parliament being dissolved and a new government taking office.[12] Ahmed's administration was different in that it was backed by the military, banned political competition for almost two years, enacted a whole raft of anti-corruption legislation and arrested a number of high profile politicians from both the AL and BNP on corruption charges. The legislation it introduced certainly sounded impressive; the Criminal Procedure Code Ordinance, for example, was amended in February 2007 – something that had been postponed more than 20 times since 1999 – to institutionalise the separation of powers between the judiciary and executive; a Financial Intelligence Unit (FIU) was set up in March 2007 with the aim of 'combat[ting] financial crimes' and 'retrieving assets and money laundered overseas' while the Electoral Commission's remit was re-written in February 2007 with the aim of 'creating a more equal playing field free from corruption'.[13] In what was an extremely hectic February, the caretaker government also acceded to the United Nations Convention against Corruption (UNCAC). And all of this policy-development despite the constitution stating that a caretaker government was normally 'not empowered to take any policy decisions' at all and limited to no more than 90 days in office.[14]

Impressive though the legislation and the array of newly empowered bodies looked on paper, the most eye-catching part of the campaign was undoubtedly the arrest of many of Bangladesh's most well-known and influential politicians. The arrests went right to the top, including both party leaders (Khaleda Zia and Sheikh Hasina), former cabinet members, leading business people and tens of thousands of others on charges that ranged from buying undue influence to bribery, tax evasion, embezzlement and fraud.[15] This was the highest profile part of what the caretaker government claimed was going to be a cleansing of Bangladeshi public life and with it the onset of a new era.

Many Bangladeshis initially welcomed these drastic measures. Indeed, many western diplomats also made it clear that 'they had no qualms in welcoming a period of military-technocratic rule' as without such an intervention there existed a real danger of the country lurching into a 'violent bloodbath'.[16] Bangladeshis had long since become tired of their country's dysfunctional politics and were hopeful that getting rid of those who were perceived to have created a system with entrenched corruption would signal a new beginning. Many of the reforms undertaken by the caretaker government were also clearly long overdue, and a wide array of pre-2007 government bodies, national and international development agencies and most prominently civil society groups had called for democratic consolidation based on very similar sets of proposals. For once, it appeared that action rather than warm words really was the order of the day. However, once the caretaker government began arresting predominant critics (most obviously those based at universities) for supposedly 'fomenting political unrest' the anti-corruption campaign began to quickly unravel.[17] Indeed, reports surfaced of 'widespread torture' of those arrested as well as of 'deaths in custody'.[18] Under these conditions, citizens rapidly grew uneasy with both the anti-corruption drive and the government itself. The notion that a military-based caretaker government could use force to compel people not to be corrupt rapidly lost any traction that it may initially have had.

Furthermore, the very same political leaders that were now imprisoned had not previously been living in a vacuum. They had always ensured that they delivered to their most important constituencies and to powerful sets of vested interests, and those people soon began to express their dissatisfaction with the actions of the caretaker administration. The lawyers empowered to bring convictions against these politicians subsequently found it increasingly difficult to convict many of those who had been arrested, largely as crucial evidence that could have been provided by those with relationships to, and interests that were aligned with, the political elite was not forthcoming. The vast majority of anti-corruption cases (including those of both party leaders) ultimately collapsed, further illustrating that without a sound understanding of the key drivers of corruption and the structures and processes that underpin it, high profile campaigns in states with low quality governance are unlikely to be successful.[19]

The radical nature of the caretaker government's approach undoubtedly has its roots in the wholly ineffective anti-corruption efforts of previous administrations. Even where substantive policy was forthcoming, it was ineffectual. And it is precisely this ineffectiveness that saw Bangladesh slip to the very bottom of TI's CPI. In February 2004, for example, Khaleda Zia's administration set up an Independent Anti-Corruption Commission (IACC). The IACC theoretically had wide-ranging powers, including the right to investigate any public official if allegations of corruption were raised against him or her. Furthermore, the IACC did not have to seek government permission to do this. In practice, however, the IACC was ineffectual. It was regularly accused of pro-government bias and all of its three (government-appointed) commissioners were criticised for their 'lack of commitment'.[20] Their work was seriously compromised by IACC's statutes which prevented it from accessing the records of banks and financial institutes, from calling for the foreign exchange transactions of those suspected of money laundering and of putting the affairs of multinational corporations under the microscope. Add to this the fact that the national government controlled both its budget and its administration then it should hardly come as a surprise that the IACC lacked any teeth.[21]

The caretaker government unsurprisingly reconstituted the IACC and on 22nd February 2007 all of the original commissioners were replaced. The IACC quickly became 'hyperactive', playing a significant role in helping the caretaker government launch the anti-corruption campaign discussed above.[22] The AL government that won the election of 2008 none the less claimed to want to make reforming the IACC a key priority, although the main thrust of their reform proposals involved 'imposing executive control over the commission'.[23] This became clear when in April 2010 the government approved a raft of amendments including the need for the IACC to receive government permission before taking any action against a public official. NGOs such as TIB were not slow in publicly criticising many of these amendments in detail.[24]

With the benefit of hindsight, it would appear that much of the high profile anti-corruption fanfare of 2007 and 2008 has had little lasting impact. The AL's anti-corruption rhetoric post-2008, meanwhile, has a strong and at times overt party political dimension to it. Fakhruddin's interim government set itself an implausibly large number of grand goals, and, as time went by, many in the administration admitted that fulfilling any, let alone all, of them was going to be very difficult. As calls for a return to democratic government became ever louder, the caretaker government ultimately handed power back in early 2009 and in doing so it struck a series of compromises with Bangladeshi's key party political actors. The same leaders are now back at the top of the same parties that continue to be as bitterly opposed as they were before.

Where top down policies have proven successful, then the success has been relative; this is not to talk it down, in a country as corruption-ridden as Bangladesh any progress is to be welcomed. The judiciary and the executive are now indeed more independent of one another than at any time in Bangladeshi history, but cases – such as that of Muhammad Yunus, a Nobel-Prize winning founder of a micro-lending bank who was forced to retire on a technicality after falling out with Sheikh Hasina, and also the war-crimes trials of 2011 that curiously only seem to be interested in putting opposition politicians in the dock – do arise that give serious cause for concern.[25] The electoral commission has performed a minor miracle not just in creating a reliable electoral register but also in getting the parties to comply with its registration demands, but many of the rules (particularly to do with funding) which apparently govern party and electoral competition are still more or less flagrantly flouted. Progress has, however, been made, and the electoral commission's secret is that it always made it clear that it wanted to work with the parties where possible rather than against them. Bangladesh's Right to Information Act (effective from 1 July 2009) was described as no less than 'epoch-making' by Prime Minister Hasina, whilst the Whistleblower Act (enacted on 6th June 2011) also looks a more promising tool for protecting those who want to report incidences of corruption than anything that existed before.[26] Whether this legislation will help to fundamentally change Bangladesh's culture of corruption remains to be seen.

Bottom up anti-corruption attempts

The nature and impact of bottom-up anti-corruption reforms will by definition be completely different to those instituted in the corridors of power in Dhaka. These responses are likely to be piecemeal, small-scale and predominantly with the aim of changing patterns of behaviour and ways of thinking on the ground. They also require the commitment and dedication of people who can have much to lose if they antagonise those in powerful positions.

Transparency International Bangladesh (TIB) has been by a distance the most prominent in pushing bottom up policies that it hopes will coax and cajole citizens into internalising non-corrupt practices. TIB was founded in 1994 and by 2010 it had 249 staff, of whom 119 were based at its head office in Dhaka.[27] Initially, TIB encountered widespread cynicism about its ability to influence processes of corruption.[28] By the late 2000s it had nonetheless developed a range of initiatives that were slowly empowering people to tackle the worst excesses of corruption in their state.[29] These initiatives were basically threefold.

Firstly, it was helping 'committees of concerned citizens' (CCCs) to develop and act as 'local level anti-corruption watchdogs'.[30] In 2000 six such committees existed, by 2010 the number had risen to 45.[31] CCC members' short-term aim is to transmit the need for transparent and accountable decision-making in local politics and service delivery. Their long-term aim is to gradually expand the number of people who embrace, and act upon, principles of non-corrupt practice. Whilst CCCs will never be able to oversee all transactions between state officials and private citizens, the aim is to set a clear marker and to develop 'a social movement driven by volunteers who challenge the notion that corruption could be a way of life'.[32]

Secondly, TIB has developed a broad network of advice centres, mobile information desks and 'face-the-public' programmes. The centres and desks, around which 195 events took place in 2009, help citizens gain information on both the obligations of state officials towards them as well as their own individual rights. The same can be said for the 34 'face-the-public' events, where local government representatives met members of the public to answer their questions[33] as well as the 24 'Information Fairs' that took place in 2010.[34] In 2010 TIB even sent text messages to more than 60 million Bangladeshis advising them to 'say no to corruption' and an 'anti-corruption theme song' (*Jago Manush* – Rise up People) is now available to download as a ring-tone.[35] Suspiciously gimmicky though one or two of these activities may be, these events, which TIB estimated (leaving text messages and downloads to one side) reached about 125,000 people in total, are subsequently seen by TIB as a useful way of drawing citizens into the anti-corruption movement.[36]

Thirdly, TIB has encouraged the development of 'Youth Engagement and Support' (YES) groups. They are attached to CCCs and tend to have a membership of between 15 and 30. They, too, principally aim to raise awareness, and they are subsequently free to shape their agendas around the particular challenges they see in their own local government administration, hospitals and schools (the three areas that tend to get particular emphasis). The number of individuals that are actively involved in these initiatives remains small (around 5,200 in 2010), but TI rightly claims that one has to start somewhere. In practice, this tends to mean persuading institutions – schools, hospitals and so on – to act as 'islands of integrity', signing an integrity pledge stating that employees will not accept bribes, will make agreed sets of information public and will generally act in an honest and open manner at all times. Eleven of these pledges, which TI describes as 'a micro level social accountability process ... to promote participatory and accountable governance at the level of service delivery by a voluntary engagement of stakeholders' and have the status of a legally non-binding social contracts, were signed in 2009, for example, whilst six were signed in 2010 taking the total to 24.[37] The CCCs and YES groups can then look to hold the signatories to this and call them (publicly) to account if they fall short of the pledges made. Colin Knox highlights how TIB aims to target public officials in local governments (Union Parishad), with the aim of making them 'accountable and transparent to all service users for the range of functions' that they provide.[38]

Approaching the issue of tackling corruption by analysing micro-level activity is a long game, and substantial changes in behaviour will only really become evident years down the line. However, there is already some evidence that these bottom up approaches are bearing fruit. For one thing, TIB has started to make enemies, and this is likely to be a sign that vested interests are beginning to feel threatened. Indeed, three defamation cases were lodged against TIB in 2010, each as a result of the household survey that it conducted that year.[39] TIB has none the less claimed that specific improvements at the grassroots level have also come about on account of, for example, its system of integrity pledges. Unauthorised payments for services have, it claims, been reduced and a growing number of officials have committed to engaging stakeholders more in terms of service quality and distribution.[40]

Corruption in Kenya

Whilst Bangladesh's story is one of (small) chinks of light appearing at the end of a (long and winding) tunnel, the situation in Kenya is arguably not even that good. In early 2012 Kenya was governed by an uneasy alliance between President Mwai Kibaki and Prime Minister Raila Odinga. The power-sharing agreement that they signed on 28th February 2008 brought an internationally mediated end to the horrific violence that marred the previous election held on 27th December 2007. Not even overwhelming support for a new constitution – supported by over two-thirds of Kenyans in a referendum on 4th August 2010 – may be enough to ensure that violence does not occur again.[41] Indeed, the uneasy truce between Kibaki's Party of National Unity (PNU) and Obinga's Orange Democratic Movement (ODM) may not last through 2012, when the next round of presidential and prime ministerial elections are scheduled.

The most recent tensions in Kenyan politics are nothing new; the country gained independence from the UK in 1962, but it remained a one party state until 1991. The onset of multi-party politics did nothing to change the essentially neo-patrimonial concentration of power in the hands of the president and the maintenance of systematic sets of patron-client relationships between leaders and followers.[42] This has led Lillian Cherotich to claim that Kenyan multi-party democracy 'is nothing but a pale shadow of its predecessor, the one party state'.[43] The new 2010 constitution none the less gives the appearance of at least attempting to challenge the old dynamics by watering down the president's power, beefing up the power of parliament, making significant changes to the judiciary and also introducing a bill of rights.[44] Whether these recent reforms will actually be translated into practice remains very much to be seen.

Kenya's post-independence polity has become riddled with corruption. Transparency International Kenya states that corruption has reached 'endemic proportions', whilst Lando Ogwang describes it as 'pervasive' with many Kenyans seeking public office 'with the specific motive of looting public resources'.[45] The conclusion of the African Peer Review Mechanism's 2006 report on Kenya states that corruption 'pervades the executive, legislature, judiciary and military, as well as the civil service', summing the situation up presciently.[46] Similar statements can be found in more or less every analysis of Kenyan politics and the effect is evident if one looks at TI's CPI data for Kenya during the period 1998–2011.

Given that it is seen to be so pervasive, it is no surprise that corruption in Kenya takes many of the traditional forms. James Gathii puts these forms into three (very broad) categories; petty corruption, grand corruption and out and out looting.[47] Kenyans certainly feel the impact of petty, day-to-day corruption almost as much as Bangladeshis do, with public servants consistently demanding extra payments either for simply providing the most basic of services, for 'speeding up' bureaucratic processes or in the name of arbitrary, extra levies. This is well illustrated if one analyses any of Transparency International's regular surveys on bribery across East Africa. In Kenya the police are consistently believed to be the most corrupt institution in society – indeed, in 2011 the Kenyan police was seen as the most corrupt institution in all of East Africa – with a majority

Table 3.6   Kenya's performance in Transparency International's Corruption Perceptions Index, 1998–2011

Year	Score	Rank
1998	2.5	74 (out of 85)
1999	2.0	90 (out of 99)
2000	2.1	82 (out of 90)
2001	2.0	84 (out of 91)
2002	1.9	96 (out of 102)
2003	1.9	122 (out of 133)
2004	2.1	129 (out of 146)
2005	2.1	144 (out of 159)
2006	2.2	142 (out of 163)
2007	2.1	150 (out of 180)
2008	2.1	147 (out of 180)
2009	2.2	146 (out of 180)
2010	2.1	154 (out of 178)
2011	2.2	154 (out of 183)

Source: Transparency International's Website

of respondents regularly reporting that they themselves have had to indulge in corrupt transactions with them. In 2011, for example, 67 per cent of people in Kenya reported that 'their interactions with the police were tainted with bribery demands'.[48] The survey also revealed that more than a quarter of all bribes paid in Kenya went to the police.

Stories of grand corruption and the looting of the state are also legion, and despite the exhortations of external organisations such as the World Bank the IMF – both of which threatened, and in one case actually refused, to release money to Kenya until something was done about these processes – they remain fundamental parts of Kenyan political life.[49] Indeed, the need to finance party competition in competitive elections has led to 'an explosion of grand corruption' as those in power desperately seek to ensure that they have the resources to ensure that they stay there.[50] The infamous cases of the Anglo-Leasing Scandal that became public in 2004 and the Goldenberg Affair[51] of the early 1990s are prime examples of this, illustrating how 'big men in control of the executive use fictional front companies to appropriate funds for personal and political uses'.[52]

Tackling corruption in Kenya

Much as is the case in Bangladesh, attempts to tackle corruption have – on paper at least – none the less not been in short supply. Regular claims by politicians that they were going to stamp out corruption have led to what Lando Ogwang describes as a 'long, tortuous and inauspicious flirtation with antidotes to corruption'.[53] At times, these flirtations have been blatant and periodically it has appeared as if Kenyan politics was on the verge of making genuine progress. Between 1997–2000, for example, Kenya's anti-corruption policy 'underwent major changes' as the Kenya Anti-Corruption Authority (KACA), and the national action plan that it co-ordinated, rose to prominence.[54] Founded in 1997, it didn't take long for KACA's first director, John Mwau, to court controversy by side-stepping the attorney general to prosecute four top officials for being party to a scam involving around $2.5m connected to wheat and sugar imports.[55] By October 1998 Mwau had resigned as Director, and all the KACA advisory board had followed him.[56]

A new advisory board was appointed at the beginning of 1999, and over the next 18 months the 'new KACA' – in another high point – managed at least to investigate 156 cases of which 14 came to court.[57] But any momentum generated was thwarted on account of two things; firstly, no effective legal protection was offered to potential whistleblowers, subsequently putting many off from reporting corrupt acts that could endanger their own positions and, secondly, the KACA ultimately always had to go through the attorney general if it wished to prosecute anyone.[58] And the attorney-general had already made it abundantly clear that he was prepared to go against the KACA if needs be.

The history of the KACA was ultimately brought to an abrupt end before it had had any real chance to consolidate itself, the constitutional court declaring in December 2000 that the KACA was over-stepping its brief in attempting to prosecute people and was therefore unconstitutional. Rather than recommending reforms, the court simply banned the KACA altogether, leaving many to conclude that the judiciary had been leant on largely on account of KACA's increasing political influence.[59] An Anti-Corruption Police Unit (ACPU) replaced the KACA, but it, as its name suggests, was based within the police – an institution that was widely known to indulge in corrupt practices and very little hope was subsequently placed in the ACPU acting in an independent fashion.

The ACPU did not, however, have a particularly long life either, and in 2003, with Mwai Kibaki having replaced Daniel Arap Moi as President, the government tried to give the impression that it was taking the initiative in fighting corruption. The 'Anti-Corruption and Economic Crimes Act' (ACECA) established a new anti-corruption commission (KACC) and the government announced that it (the commission) would be the principal body tasked to co-ordinate and implement anti-corruption efforts. A further series of policy measures were also passed with some fanfare; a Public Officer Ethics Act was enacted with the aim of outlining what was and wasn't acceptable ethical behaviour when serving in public office, plus a series of specialised anti-corruption courts were created. A number of further acts entered the statute book with the aim of bringing in more transparency and accountability to the management of public affairs (the most obvious of these being the Public Audit Act, the Privatisation Act and a Procurement and Disposal Bill). Finally, a Serious Crime Unit within the Department of Public Prosecutions was also created and in 2003 Kenya signed up to the United Nation's Convention against Corruption and the African Union's Anti-Corruption Convention.[60]

Impressive though this flurry of activity sounds, in reality it was a smokescreen to give the old processes that underpinned politics a veneer of respectability. The emergence of the Anglo-leasing scandal was perfect evidence of this. On closer inspection, many parts of the various Acts mentioned above remained ambiguous, enabling those in power to get round their more awkward provisions relatively easily when required. A prime example of this concerned the Public Officer Ethics Act, which amongst other things required public servants to disclose their own personal assets. Firstly, it was not clear what information needed to be declared, and even then all declarations were to be kept confidential. Hardly the type of legislation that will reveal how wealthy many of the Kenyan elite have become.

The KACC, too, proved ineffectual. Its lack of prosecutorial powers not only led to very few convictions (by the end of 2008 it had only managed 37, whilst in 2011 this number had slipped back to 27; none of whom were high-ranking officials),[61] but also left it open to political influence. Its reputation was further tarnished when three of its own staff were fired for corruption-related offences in June 2008. Furthermore, the proliferation of institutions, policies and not least government pronouncements could not hide the fact that for ordinary Kenyans very little appeared to be changing. Indeed, the well-known and highly publicised case of John Githongo, the former head of the department of governance and ethics who resigned in January 2005 after two years in post, illustrates just how difficult it can be to fight corruption in these circumstances. Revelations of massive corruption by the Kibaki administration prompted those around the president to move against Githongo, and on realising his task – of raising ethical standards in government – was ultimately going to be thwarted at every step he not only stepped down but fled the country to live in self-imposed exile in the UK.[62] In Kenya institutional remits continued to over-lap, causing confusion and spawning a myriad of ways for those accused of corrupt acts to wriggle out of difficult corners. The government's much vaunted anti-corruption campaigns were in reality haphazard affairs that appeared to lack a core based on transparency, accountability and a willingness to get at underlying processes. Much of the legislation passed subsequently included loopholes and vagueness that again could be used by those with something to hide. In other words, Kenyan politicians and the institutions that are supposed to investigate corruption are, in the words of Teresa Omondi of TI Kenya, 'good at talking about corruption cases, but not at prosecuting anyone in them'.[63]

Issues of corruption slipped down the pecking order in the period after Githongo's departure, particularly when violence erupted both before and after the 2007 presidential and parliamentary elections. Around 1,500 Kenyans died, further emphasising the extent to which politicians – six of whom were summonsed to the International Criminal Court in December 2010 for their role in insighting the carnage – were prepared to go to extreme limits to preserve their positions of power and influence.[64] In this climate, the fight against corruption inevitably loses much of its political salience. Having said that, Aaron Ringera's re-appointment as the KACC's Director in August 2009 did lead to considerable public protest, and not just on account of the president blatantly not following the rules of procedure when re-appointing him.[65] The fact that no senior officials had been prosecuted during Ringera's first five year term of office infuriated many and ultimately led to the Kenyan parliament over-ruling the president – in and of itself a novum in Kenyan politics – and rejecting his nomination. Ringera eventually resigned on 30th September 2009.[66]

By December 2010 well-placed officials in the finance department were revealing that the country could be losing as much as third of its national budget every year to corruption, amounting to around $4bn annually.[67] The Kenyan government itself admitted that between 2005 and 2009 up to $47m had been stolen by corrupt officials in the education and health departments.[68] With very little progress being made, the KACC – in what was effectively the fourth reorganisation of the country's major anti-corruption institution in ten years – was replaced in August 2011 with an 'Ethics and Anti-Corruption Commission' (EACC). The Ethics and Anti-Corruption Act of 2011 claims that the EACC will be 'independent' and exists to enforce Chapter 6 of the new constitution on leadership and integrity.[69] Whether this happens in practice remains to be seen, but the fact that, amongst other things, the EACC can still only recommend prosecutions to the Attorney General (as opposed to actively pursuing them itself) leaves even the most optimistic of observers doubtful that much will change as a result of its creation.

The rhetoric and periodic splurges of action in Kenya appear to have done very little indeed to change the underlying corrupt processes and networks that have dominated Kenyan politics since independence. None of the anti-corruption initiatives pinpointed in Table 2.1 have been pursued with any enthusiasm or effectiveness, and many of the things that the literature explicitly states are *unlikely to work* are precisely the initiatives that have been undertaken. The repeated failures of Kenya's anti-corruption agencies are a case in point, but the often arcane, convoluted and ambiguous policies introduced have not helped either. The fact that the 2010 constitution has significantly empowered parliament vis-à-vis the president offers some hope that the still-considerable discretionary powers of the executive may slowly be reined in. The new constitution has also seen the judiciary experience something of an overhaul, with all incumbent judges resigning and the workings of the police undergoing reform.[70] There have also been moves towards devolving power to the regions, something that may or may not make tackling corruption easier.[71] A much discussed Freedom of

Information law – something that the new constitution explicitly calls on the government to pass – was proposed on 15th August 2011, and if it is ultimately passed and implemented in anything like the manner foreseen, it will offer more for anti-corruption activists to work with. Kenyans do at least now have an open data portal, launched on 8th July 2011, making the Kenyan government 'the first African country to release government data to the public through a single platform'.[72] The ripple effects of the new constitution subsequently do look like an improvement on its predecessor. However, given the evidence over the last decade, it would none the less be a brave person who expected corruption in Kenyan politics to be fundamentally undermined any time soon.

Lessons from Bangladesh and Kenya

The analysis of anti-corruption attempts in Kenya and Bangladesh reveals a number of things. Firstly, without 'buy in' from prominent stakeholders top-down attempts to cleanse public life are destined not just to fail but to fail badly. This is nothing new. The only rays of sunlight in this area come when newly empowered institutions successfully manage to walk the tightrope that links their ideals with the interests of the political actors they are trying to influence. The partial success of Bangladesh's electoral commission is a good indicator of how this can work in practice. Persuading all parties to comply with registration requirements was certainly a considerable achievement, and there can be little doubt that they acceded to this demand because the commission sought dialogue and adopted what Nizam Ahmed defines as a 'participatory strategy'.[73] Adopting a Right to Information Act in 2009, a Whistleblower Protection Act in 2011, and establishing both an Information Commission in 2009 and a Human Rights Commission (in 2007) have, despite the difficulties in actually implementing the provisions in them, also clearly been steps in the right direction.

Meanwhile in Kenya, the last decade has been one of plentiful anti-corruption talk and disappointingly little anti-corruption substance. Kenya's political elite brought in a raft of anti-corruption legislation, but precious little changed in terms of levels of perceptions of corruption. Indeed, the cynicism with which Kenyans view the political process remained as obvious as ever. The introduction of a new constitution in 2010 may offer a ray of hope, and some of the changes, whilst not framed in anti-corruption language, may have a more sustainable impact on corruption in practice. The President's discretionary powers have been limited and Parliament's willingness to stand up to the president by rejecting Aaron Ringera's re-nomination as head of the KACC is certainly evidence that something has changed. Moves towards Freedom of Information, whilst still only tentative, also look much more promising than much of the anti-corruption legislation that was passed over the last decade.

It is also worth noting that although TIB's enthusiastic attempts to help the general public in Bangladesh gain a stake in society – through creating CCCs, YES groups and also via devices such as Integrity Pledges and via a variety of campaigns – were never likely to change Bangladesh overnight they were noteworthy. From little acorns do great oak trees grow, and the increasing visibility of their activities, plus the fact that a number of vested interests have – largely unsuccessfully – began challenging TIB indicates that progress is being made. The steps are small, but they are steps none the less. Kenya would do well to learn from these developments.

The small improvements that Bangladesh is perceived to have made in both the CPI and WGI ('controlling corruption') data should, however, not be over-stressed. When margins of error and other potential influences on the data (as discussed in Chapter 2) are taken into account, then it is clear progress should be measured in feet and inches rather than miles. However, qualitative analysis of the Bangladesh case does back up the Bangladeshi Daily Star's tentative December 2011 conclusion that the country 'is at least inching forward'.[74] And that has to be something. Kenya, meanwhile, made no progress at all through the 2000s, and this despite public claims that tackling corruption was a high priority. In fact, the story in Kenya is as depressing as it was predictable. However, providing that Kenya can see out 2012 without lurching back into violence (a big 'if', admittedly), then the new constitution and the acts that claim to want to protect those reporting corruption, to limit discretionary power and also to disseminate reliable information on the behaviour of public servants would appear to be on the right lines. But history tells us to be wary of expecting too much.

4
South Korea and Poland: Tough Talk, Small Steps, Contested Outcomes

Introduction

The situations of South Korea and Poland are very different to those of Bangladesh and Kenya. As in the latter two states, corruption remains a prominent feature of public discourse in both South Korea and Poland, but it has not prevented both states from making, at times, impressive economic progress. This is not to say that corruption *facilitated* economic development, but it certainly did not throttle growth in the way that it has done in many states around the world and, indeed, in the way that much of the traditional literature on corruption says that it should. The literature on the effects of corruption has subsequently been (somewhat paradoxically) enriched by the apparently awkward cases of states such as South Korea (and some of its East Asian neighbours) and Poland.[1]

One key thing that both South Korea and Poland do possess is a fair degree of what one might call 'governance competence'. And this is significant. The quality of governance is certainly mixed, and both South Korea and Poland perform well in some areas and less well in others. It has not, however, been an outright block on economic development. Both states have subsequently created models that have enabled significant levels of corruption to go hand-in-hand with economic growth. Eventually, however, the built-in costs that systemic corruption engenders come back to haunt even those states that enjoy significant periods of progress. In South Korea's case this was more obvious than most as when the Asian economic crisis of the late 1990s hit, South Korea was badly affected. The challenge is therefore not to fundamentally overhaul governance structures, but to work out what works, why, what doesn't and what can be done to counteract it within each particular governance context. Only then will the challenge of dealing with corruption be faced down.

At first glance, Poland and South Korea might appear to be very different social, economic, cultural and political environments. Yet on closer inspection there are a number of good reasons to compare and contrast their respective performances in attempting (or not, as the case may be) to tackle corruption. First and foremost, both countries have emerged relatively recently (1987 in the case of South Korea and 1989 in the case of Poland) from extended periods of non-democratic rule. Both are now multi-party democracies. Both are politically stable and reasonably well-off, both have histories of colonial domination and have undergone impressive processes of socio-economic transformation. Persistent claims that public life remains overtly politicised are also regularly made. Regimes in both countries have also periodically launched high-profile anti-corruption drives. There are therefore good reasons for comparing and contrasting their performances in terms of tackling corruption.

As with the cases of Bangladesh and Kenya, it is worth looking at WGI data to give a feel for the specific type of governance challenge that these two states face. The data in Tables 4.1 and 4.2 cover the same six governance indicators across the same period as was the case with Bangladesh and Kenya (1996–2002). Again, as in the previous chapter, the percentile rank illustrates how both countries faired in comparison with other countries. The next column reveals the governance score per indicator per year. A score of zero would indicate a position where half of the other countries performed better on average for that indicator, whilst half performed worse, with scores of –2.5 and +2.5 being the respective (bad and good) ends of the spectrum. Importantly, the standard errors are also included here, indicating how robust the data is.

As is to be expected, we see variety across indicators and also across time within individual indicators. Although these data do not, and cannot, give us a complete picture, we do nonetheless see at least some sort of indication that the quality of governance during this period has been reasonably good. Both states appear to have left their non-democratic heritage behind and to have created regimes that are able to carry out policy effectively and to provide an environment where citizens can feel safe, secure and able to act freely. In contrast to both Bangladesh and Kenya, both South Korea and Poland register scores that consistently – across time and indicator – place them in the top of half of states in terms of governance

Table 4.1   The quality of governance in South Korea, 1996–2002

Governance Indicator	Sources	Year	Percentile Rank (0–100)	Governance Score (−2.5 – +2.5)	Standard Error
Voice and Accountability	9	2002	70.2	+0.73	0.17
	7	2000	67.3	+0.61	0.21
	6	1998	66.8	+0.60	0.23
	6	1996	69.2	+0.70	0.22
Political Stability	6	2002	47.6	+0.14	0.28
	5	2000	54.3	+0.19	0.30
	4	1998	60.1	+0.40	0.32
	4	1996	62.5	+0.47	0.36
Government Effectiveness	7	2002	79.5	+0.89	0.17
	6	2000	76.6	+0.75	0.19
	6	1998	64.4	+0.32	0.19
	5	1996	72.2	+0.63	0.23
Regulatory Quality	8	2002	75.0	+0.78	0.20
	7	2000	69.1	+0.55	0.21
	7	1998	58.8	+0.26	0.25
	6	1996	64.2	+0.38	0.27
Rule of Law	10	2002	77.0	+0.92	0.17
	9	2000	77.5	+0.86	0.15
	8	1998	72.7	+0.76	0.19
	7	1996	73.7	+0.80	0.20
Control of Corruption	7	2002	69.8	+0.46	0.16
	7	2000	65.4	+0.29	0.18
	7	1998	65.4	+0.33	0.16
	6	1996	64.9	+0.26	0.18

Source: http://info.worldbank.org/governance/wgi/sc_chart.asp# viewed on 15th August 2012

Table 4.2   The quality of governance in Poland, 1996–2002

Governance Indicator	Sources	Year	Percentile Rank (0–100)	Governance Score (−2.5 − +2.5)	Standard Error
Voice and	9	2002	81.7	+1.07	0.17
Accountability	7	2000	81.7	+1.04	0.21
	6	1998	80.3	+1.04	0.23
	6	1996	78.4	+1.01	0.22
Political	6	2002	64.9	+0.62	0.28
Stability	5	2000	56.3	+0.26	0.30
	4	1998	69.7	+0.67	0.32
	4	1996	71.6	+0.76	0.36
Government	8	2002	68.8	+0.49	0.17
Effectiveness	7	2000	73.2	+0.58	0.19
	6	1998	75.1	+0.60	0.19
	5	1996	76.1	+0.73	0.23
Regulatory	10	2002	73.0	+0.72	0.19
Quality	9	2000	71.6	+0.63	0.20
	8	1998	70.1	+0.61	0.23
	7	1996	72.5	+0.69	0.26
Rule of Law	12	2002	68.9	+0.62	0.16
	11	2000	69.9	+0.63	0.15
	9	1998	72.2	+0.76	0.18
	8	1996	69.4	+0.69	0.18
Control of	8	2002	66.8	+0.33	0.15
Corruption	8	2000	70.2	+0.47	0.18
	7	1998	76.6	+0.66	0.17
	5	1996	72.7	+0.54	0.23

Source: http://info.worldbank.org/governance/wgi/sc_chart.asp# viewed on 15th August 2012

quality. That is not to deny that both states face significant governance challenges, but they are starting from altogether different positions to that of Bangladesh and Kenya. Indeed, the nearest that either of the countries came to slipping in to the bottom half in terms of their governance scores came in 2002, when South Korea dipped to 0.14 in terms of political stability.

In general, this is more or less as most South Korea and Poland watchers will have expected. We do nonetheless see variation here, ranging from performances that are barely above average ('political stability' in South Korea in 2002) through to some good performances (such as 'voice and accountability' in Poland across more or less the whole period in question). Poland's performances generally outperform those of South Korea, although even then the pattern is not consistent (South Korea comes out better in terms of 'rule of law' across the whole time frame, for example).

The story of governance quality is, of course, naturally one of nuance, and we find plenty of evidence to illustrate that here. Given that Poland, for example, has developed into a thriving multi-party democracy, it scores consistently well in the area of 'voice and accountability' – South Korea lags behind here. South Korea has, on the other hand, out-performed Poland in terms of the 'rule of law', whilst neither country appears to have come out particularly well (in comparison with other nominally developed states) in terms of 'political stability'. The overall picture is subsequently one of two states where governance quality is generally good, even though there is room for improvement across the board.

In terms of 'control of corruption', the data is particularly interesting.[2] The data in Tables 4.3 and 4.4 spans not just the period from 1996–2002, but has also been brought up to 2010. In the case of South Korea, the data appears to indicate that there has been a gradual improvement in the government's attempts to control corruption, but progress has been slow. The data in Table 4.5 on South Korea's CPI scores over the same period generally backs this up, with noticeable improvements in performance from the mid-2000s. Given the importance of taking measurement errors into account, it is probably best to assume that although progress has been patchy, uneven and quite possibly contested in some parts, it nonetheless appears that South Korea has been moving forwards rather than backwards.

The picture for Poland is similar. The high standard error measurements for the scores in the late 1990s and early 2000s (Table 4.4) need to be noted, but even then the score of 0.14 for 2004 looks much different from 0.41 and 0.45 that Poland achieved in the two

Table 4.3   Control of corruption, South Korea, 1996–2010

Country	Sources	Year	Percentile Rank (0–100)	Governance Score (–2.5 – +2.5)	Standard Error
South Korea	12	2010	69.4	+0.42	0.14
	12	2009	70.8	+0.46	0.14
	11	2008	68.9	+0.42	0.14
	11	2007	72.8	+0.54	0.14
	11	2006	67.3	+0.32	0.14
	9	2005	71.2	+0.61	0.14
	9	2004	66.3	+0.36	0.15
	8	2003	71.7	+0.49	0.16
	7	2002	69.8	+0.46	0.16
	7	2000	65.4	+0.29	0.18
	7	1998	65.4	+0.33	0.16
	6	1996	64.9	+0.26	0.18

Source: WGI data, accessed 15th August 2012

Table 4.4   Control of corruption, Poland, 1996–2010

Country	Sources	Year	Percentile Rank (0–100)	Governance Score (–2.5 – +2.5)	Standard Error
Poland	13	2010	70.3	+0.45	0.13
	13	2009	69.9	+0.41	0.14
	13	2008	67.5	+0.33	0.13
	12	2007	60.7	+0.19	0.13
	12	2006	61.0	+0.18	0.13
	10	2005	62.0	+0.23	0.13
	10	2004	60.0	+0.14	0.14
	9	2003	68.3	+0.37	0.14
	8	2002	66.8	+0.33	0.15
	8	2000	70.2	+0.47	0.18
	7	1998	76.6	+0.66	0.17
	5	1996	72.7	+0.54	0.23

Source: WGI data, accessed 15th August 2012

most recent years available (2009 and 2010). Poland's CPI scores point in a similar direction (Table 4.6), with the years 2003–2006 being particular low points, before improvements were made in the late 2000s and then in to the first decade of the 21st century. The fact in the early and mid-2000s the issue of corruption became highly salient in elections for both the national parliament and the presidency is likely to have had an impact here, and this is something that is discussed in more detail below.

The fact that the data for South Korea and Poland would appear to be more encouraging than was the case for Bangladesh and Kenya has not stopped politicians in the former from periodically launching initiatives to try and root corruption out. In many ways, these initiatives have been every bit as high-profile and contentious as were those that were discussed in Chapter 3, and corruption has rarely been too far away from the top of policy agendas. Given what we know about anti-corruption programmes and governance regimes, and as was discussed on pages 42–45 and in Table 2.1, the following broadly defined anti-corruption mechanisms would appear to be at least worth considering, and all were in some shape or form, in both countries discussed here:

- to sharpen up democratic oversight procedures
- to increase the accountability of civil servants' actions
- to disentangle, and increase the transparency of, the relationships between business elites and political elites
- to give the media genuine teeth to investigate alleged incidences of corrupt or inappropriate behaviour.[3]

The rest of this chapter will analyse the key successes and failures evident in each state. Again, this is not a list-making exercise, and the aim of the case study analysis here is to illustrate where progress was (and was not) made and, crucially, why that was the case. Importantly, both states have taken broadly similar approaches, even if they have been understandably nuanced to reflect national circumstances – and the relative successes and failures can tell us a considerable amount about when each particular approach is more or less likely to bear fruit.

Tackling corruption in South Korea

'Controlling corruption is' according to Jong-Sung You 'a particularly difficult task for young democracies'. Indeed, empirical research indicates that it is really only 'mature and stable democracies' that remain

Table 4.5   **South Korea's performance in Transparency International's Corruption Perceptions Index, 1998–2011**

Year	Score	Rank
1998	4.3	42 (out of 85)
1999	3.8	50 (out of 99)
2000	4.0	48 (out of 90)
2001	4.2	42 (out of 91)
2002	4.5	40 (out of 102)
2003	4.3	50 (out of 133)
2004	4.5	47 (out of 146)
2005	5.0	40 (out of 159)
2006	5.1	42 (out of 163)
2007	5.1	43 (out of 180)
2008	5.6	40 (out of 180)
2009	5.5	39 (out of 180)
2010	5.4	39 (out of 178)
2011	5.4	43 (out of 183)

Source: Transparency International's Website.

significantly less corrupt than not just younger democracies but also autocratic regimes.[4] South Korea's efforts to tackle corruption since 1987 are therefore all the more noteworthy for their (relative) success, and that even if noteworthy challenges still remain.

Pre-1987 and the advent of democratic reforms, South Korea's rapid economic growth went hand-in-hand with what Michael Johnston has termed 'elite cartel corruption'.[5] For those in power through the 1960s, 1970s and 1980s, corruption was more a means of control than influence, and the key aim was 'always to protect, as well as to enrich, networks of higher-level elites'.[6] This was done by rewarding business leaders who made direct or indirect financial contributions to the pet projects (and often the political organisations) of political leaders.[7] The culture of crony capitalism that developed benefited both the politicians and the conglomerates (or 'chaebols') – just as long as those same conglomerates used their privileged positions in growth-enhancing ways. This was to become a double-edged sword; on the positive side, the chaebols 'devoted themselves' to South Korea's economic development by driving exports ever higher.[8] On the negative side, the economy became extremely centralised and bureaucratic, deterring both 'stability and [a] fair distribution of benefits'.[9] Development in South Korea was subsequently planned and strictly controlled by an authoritarian state, with resource allocation based overwhelmingly on the interests of politicians and the economic elite. By the 1980s, political and economic power became to all intents and purposes fused.[10] Furthermore, 'illicit funds and docile bureaucrats' enabled governments 'lacking in political legitimacy and popular support' to stay in power even though there was always considerable disdain for them within society.[11] The threat of force to underpin these relationships was never far from the surface. State capture was subsequently 'rampant' and bureaucratic corruption 'inevitable', as close relationships 'became absolute necessities for sustaining political power' and maintaining 'commercial success'.[12] In return for their support, chosen businesses got easy access to capital, light (or non-existent) regulation and the state ensured peaceful industrial relations.[13] Corrupt though they undoubtedly were, these relationships underpinned much of the South Korean economic success story until, at the latest, the Asian Crash of 1997.

The South Korean version of 'elite cartel corruption' traditionally had the president at the core of a network of business and military figures. Institutions were generally weak as strong personalities cultivated relationships in what Johnston called a 'continuous incentive system' where all of the 'political-business-bureaucratic network' that ran South Korea had good reason to support each other.[14] This did not necessarily make governing the country easy. Competing interests were always vying for the ear of those in power, and given that one of the criteria for being allowed into the cartel was the ability to deliver economic benefits, competition could be cutthroat. However, as Johnston again wryly notes, these difficulties notwithstanding, leading South Korea could undoubtedly be a highly lucrative business.[15]

South Korea's impressive economic progress and a culture that traditionally showed considerable deference to those in power could not shield the government indefinitely from an increasingly restive civil society. By 1987 moves were afoot to bring in more democratic forms of political competition and with it changing attitudes to the elite-cartel corruption that had existed for 35 years. South Korean governments had, of course, paid lip service to fighting corruption for decades, and a regular stream of campaigns, proclamations and new laws were, particularly when new governments came to power, forthcoming. The point of these initiatives was less to tackle the corruption that the government was very much at the core of, and much more a symbolic attempt to placate a restive population and a very practical way of removing political opponents.[16] The system, in other words, undoubtedly fostered corrupt behaviour, but the government tended, for obvious reasons, 'to focus on individual irregularities, turning a blind eye to the system and mechanisms themselves'.[17]

The first substantive reforms came under the administration of Kim Young-sam (1993–1998). Young-sam's regime enhanced the powers of the 'Board of Audit and Inspection' (BAI) and took the important step (in 1993) of bringing in a 'Real Name Transactions Act', compelling all financial accounts to be held in the real name of their owners. Given the levels of financial collusion that took place in South Korea, this step was of genuine significance, indicating a move towards more transparency and accountability.

Further substantive steps were taken in the era of Kim Dae-jung (1998–2003). Soon after becoming president his office announced its intention to develop a set of wide-ranging anti-corruption programmes. They were centred predominantly on five issues:

- the creation of a high-profile anti-corruption agency
- the promulgation of a wide-ranging and detailed law on the prevention of corruption
- increasing public awareness of where corruption was taking place and how to spot it
- the development of a campaign encouraging citizen participation in corruption detection
- to reform government and administrative procedures in areas where corruption was particularly bad.[18]

Kim Dae-jung's ideas marked a real departure in South Korean politics. For the first time in South Korea's modern history a leader appeared to be serious about tackling the endemic corruption that had long since epitomised South Korean public life. Furthermore, Kim Dae-jung made a point of trying to engage civil society in holding economic and political elites to account. He listened to organisations such as the Citizens' Coalition for Promulgating a Corruption Prevention Law (made up of 38 South Korean NGOs) and brought them in to the discussions that ultimately led to the Anti-Corruption Act of July 2001.[19] A wide variety of other NGOs were created and encouraged in their work – all with the aim of improving governance within the country.[20] Kim Dae-jung also passed a Money Laundering Prevention Act in 2001 and by 2003 his government had passed a presidential decree creating a Code of Conduct for Maintaining the Integrity of Public Officials. An anti-corruption agency – the Korea Independent Commission Against Corruption (KICAC) – also came into being in 2002. The key tenets of South Korea's current anti-corruption framework were subsequently created and developed under his leadership.

Whilst Kim Dae-jung did a great deal to beef up the institutional anti-corruption framework, real practical problems remained. Although significant changes took place in South Korea during this period, in 2001 Transparency International still noted that 'the ascendancy of collusion and illicit networks over technology and productivity has never been stronger'.[21] Bhargava and Bolongaita, in their comprehensive analysis of anti-corruption attempts in Asia, concur, adding that 'the rule-bending business culture is persistent and the implementation of corporate governance measures has not been evenly achieved'.[22] In other words, the changes made often looked more impressive on paper than they did in practice. The introduction of the KICAC was another prime example of this. It was supposed to provide a 'check and balance system' that promoted transparency and accountability.[23] In practice, the fact that it was not given investigative power meant that it was never likely to work 'as effectively as the government originally intended'.[24] So, even though gradual improvements were undoubtedly made in South Korea's national integrity system, shortcomings were still clearly in evidence.[25] Jon Quah pinpointed four particular ones, ranging from the need to introduce effective monitoring mechanisms for public officials to strengthening the commitment of the courts to enforce pre-existing anti-corruption laws, and from empowering the KICAC with more 'authoritative and/or investigative powers' to establishing a special body that would investigate corruption by high-ranking officials.[26]

As is often the case with anti-corruption agencies, the KICAC did not, in its original form, last particularly long. By 2008 it was merged with the Ombudsman and the Administrative Appeals

Commission to form the Anti-Corruption and Civil Rights Commission (ACRC). Given the KICAC's toothlessness in actually investigating incidences of corruption, there was hope that ACRC's powers would be broadened – in vain, as it turned out, as the ACRC's remit remained the same as that of the now defunct KICAC.[27] Indeed, the disappointment with which the newly formed ACRC was subsequently greeted was symptomatic of where, through the 2000s, the anti-corruption movement in South Korea found itself. As time wore on it became clear that a lot of anti-corruption background noise was in fact masking a manifest lack of political will to change things. This can be seen by the steady stream of scandals that continued to engulf the South Korean political elite, as well as the permanent suspicion that close friends and relatives as well as favoured businessmen were, and are, able to pursue 'business-as-usual' even though much of the institutional framework appears to have changed.

The restructuring of the national anti-corruption agency and the development of a framework that did allow citizens to gain more information on the activities of their public servants than ever before could not mask the fact that 'weak regulations governing conflicts of interest and asset declarations' allowed public officials to continue to skilfully use the darker areas of public life to enrich themselves (and their friends).[28] This situation prevailed despite the introduction of a much vaunted Korean Pact on Anti-Corruption and Transparency (or K-Pact) in 2005. The K-Pact was a long-term 'multi-stakeholder alliance' promoting 'the implementation of regional and sectorial anti-corruption declarations'.[29] The aim of the pact was simply to bring together public, private and civil society actors around ten principles to forge anti-corruption alliances, and by 2007, 15 such initiatives were signed.[30] Although participation was voluntary, the plan was to create a strong framework of ethically sound relationships that publically praised those who acted honourably whilst naming and shaming those who violated the pact. Building such coalitions is an important part of creating a viable integrity system, but in the cold light of day South Korea still does not monitor the personal assets of officials (particularly important when issues of procurement and privatisation are parts of their respective briefs) and the revolving door between business, governments and the middle men between them remains largely unregulated.[31] This problem is well summarised by Nathaniel Heller, the Managing

Director of Global Integrity, who argues that the importance of chaebols in South Korea's recent past should ensure that 'greater attention be paid to curbing potential conflicts of interest'. Heller argues that the only way of doing this is by promoting 'transparency around senior officials' sources of income and wealth'.[32] South Korea's system for investigating allegedly unethical, corrupt activity subsequently remains painfully unable to do this.

The validity of these observations has been backed up time and time again as corruption scandals have been unearthed. The tragic suicide of former president (2003–2008) Roh Moo-hyun is a prime example. Roh himself was never indicted for any offence, but by the time he jumped off a bridge on 24th May 2009, a close family friend, Park Yeon-cha, had been arrested on tax evasion and bribery charges, and his elder brother, Roh Geon-pyong, and a classmate from school and long-time confidant, Chung Sang-mun, were also facing bribery allegations.[33] Such scandals have been depressingly commonplace, and as recently as June 2012 President Lee Myung-bak acknowledged that the country was 'still struggling with a culture of illicit favours', which was 'rampant not only among financial regulators but also in other parts of society, ranging from the judiciary, tax authorities and military through to the civil service'.[34] He might well have included his own family and close associates in that, particularly as, in practices that echoed those of Roh, his elder brother, two other relatives and a number of his long-time aides had been arrested for bribery.[35] This is not to mention his allies' influence in promoting and appointing their supporters to other politically and economically significant positions. Mr Lee's public apology and his claim that he was 'so ashamed that I can hardly lift my face' may well have influenced the harsher judgement passed little more than two months later on the chairman of the Hanwha Group, one of the largest and most influential Chaebols, who was imprisoned for four years for various financial misdemeanors. This may, finally, be an indication that the traditional willingness to protect white collar criminals could be on the wane – as recently as 2007 the chairman of the now defunct Hyundai conglomerate was given a three year suspended prison sentence for embezzlement as the presiding judge claimed he was too important to serve time, whilst in 2008 the chairman of Samsung received a similar sentence for tax evasion. Despite resigning as Samsung's chairman, he returned to the post little more than two years later.[36] These cases are just two of dozens where businessmen who committed similar crimes received suspended sentences only to be pardoned soon after.[37]

Tackling corruption in Poland

Poland's post-1989 transformation from an authoritarian state with a planned economy to a democratic, prosperous country at the heart of the European Union has been a remarkable one. Yet since 1990 cases of corruption have been regular features of Polish public life. At one time or another the Polish president, prime minister, other senior politicians, senior civil servants and bureaucrats right through the public sector have been accused of behaving in a corrupt fashion.[38] It is impossible to provide authoritative data on the exact scale of corruption in Poland (or anywhere else for that matter), but opinion poll research has shown us that Poles have long felt that politicians have consistently and systematically enriched themselves.[39] As Aleksander Surdej has put it, 'the perception is of omnipresent corruption'.[40]

This is not, of course, to say that corruption in Poland was invented in 1989. Poles had little access to information regarding the acts of those in power during the communist era, but this did not prevent them from knowing that the system was built on a series of corrupt relationships. They also knew through experience that personal relationships, political connections and plain old bribery could be efficient and effective ways of improving their own daily lives. The end of communism may well have brought much that Polish citizens were pleased about, but removing deeply rooted patterns of corruption did not, and could not, happen overnight. Indeed, corruption has been a prevalent part of the Third Republic since its inception in 1989. In a transition period that was full of uncertainties, bribery was often considered to be a speedy and effective way around cumbersome bureaucratic procedures. The 'soft corruption of protectionism, clientelism and nepotism' were also never far from the surface as state assets were distributed to those with suitable connections.[41]

During the 1990s no government made any serious attempt to root out these corrupt practices and networks. The rhetoric was at times impressive, but the practice was not. Corruption became a 'phenomenon of a systemic nature' that looked to have deeply entrenched itself in much of public life.[42] Constant changes of government led to constant changes in bureaucratic personnel, as each government attempted to put its loyal servants in positions of influence and power. And, these party supporters knew fully what to expect as and when 'their' government lost office – they would be moved on too.[43] Given this, and 'with little understanding of how soft corruption affects a state and with no visible strategy or tools to tackle it', Poland in the 1990s became a 'vulnerable victim of corrupt activities' that began eroding the substance of its new institutional framework.[44]

Over the last decade the issue of corruption has risen significantly in political salience. Indeed, analysts of public life in Poland have moved from putting the nature, style and substance of radical economic reforms under the microscope (as was the case through the 1990s) to analysing quality of governance issues – with corruption the 'most significant indicator'.[45] Corruption, particularly in the mid-2000s, also became a 'highly politicised issue' as perceptions and allegations of corruption became ever more 'politically driven'.[46] In the words of Heywood and Meyer-Sahling, corruption moved to the 'very centre of public debate'[47] as high-profile scandals 'continued to reinforce' perceptions of sustained high-level corruption.[48] Although a number of comprehensive strategies were developed in the late-1990s to tackle corruption, the European Commission still claimed (in 2002) that corruption 'threatens to undermine the functioning of many public spheres'[49] whilst another EU Strategy Paper claimed that corruption remained a 'serious cause for concern'.[50]

As noted below, Polish governments periodically stressed how important they thought fighting corruption was, but it was not until 2000 that the 'Anti-Corruption Working Group' was set up and that anything genuinely substantive appeared to happen. This came about primarily on the back of a World Bank report on Poland in 1999 and signalled a step change in terms of the issue's popular salience.[51] On the one hand, Poland began to engage with the international community's efforts to combat corruption. The keenness of Polish elites to join the European Union saw them adopt various anti-corruption initiatives, ranging from the OECD's Convention on Combating the Bribery of Foreign Public Officials (2000) to the Council of Europe's Civil and Criminal Law Conventions (September

Table 4.6   **Poland's performance in Transparency International's Corruption Perceptions Index, 1998–2011**

Year	Score	Rank
1998	4.6	39 (out of 85)
1999	4.2	44 (out of 99)
2000	4.1	43 (out of 90)
2001	4.1	44 (out of 91)
2002	4.0	45 (out of 102)
2003	3.6	64 (out of 133)
2004	3.5	67 (out of 146)
2005	3.4	70 (out of 159)
2006	3.7	61 (out of 163)
2007	4.2	61 (out of 180)
2008	4.6	58 (out of 180)
2009	5.0	49 (out of 180)
2010	5.3	41 (out of 178)
2011	5.5	41 (out of 183)

Source: Transparency International's Website.

and December 2002). Even after Poland joined the EU, the treaty ratifying continued; the EU's Convention on the Fight against Corruption involving Officials of the European Communities or Officials of the EU Member States was ratified in January 2005 and the UN's Convention against Corruption in September 2006.[52] Impressive though these agreements sound, their immediate effectiveness remained (and remains) questionable, and many of the moves by Polish governments had 'a façade-like character'. They were more about fulfilling the criteria for joining the EU and box-ticking than genuinely combatting corrupt practices.[53]

On the other hand, the government did make a series of positive moves to tackle corruption. The first anti-corruption strategy was revealed in 2002 – indeed, this was originally heralded as a 'flagship anti-corruption undertaking'[54] – whilst between 2002 and 2005 numerous changes were made to the legal code so as to tighten up anti-corruption legislation.[55] The 2002 strategy was target-based and supposed to help administrative departments root out corrupt practices. In general terms, its three main aims were to promote ethically sound practices within government, to increase the effectiveness of detection and to increase public awareness of where corruption was most likely to be found. Amongst many other things, the strategy encouraged ministries to bring in anti-corruption training, to disseminate information on ethically sound procedures and to think about best (and worst) practices. Each ministry had to implement the specific tasks set by the end of the 2003.[56]

Fulfilling the wide and at times diverse aims of the strategy inevitably proved difficult, and the Batory Foundation argues that around 30 per cent of the programme had been 'delayed' beyond the deadline whilst several of the key tasks were not even addressed.[57] Many of the tasks were also deceptively general in nature, and appeared more suitable for persuading European Union monitors (an organisation Poland was very enthusiastic about joining) than for actually getting to the root of the problem. Furthermore, some departments took a 'purely formal' approach to achieving their anti-corruption goals and much of their activities either lacked genuine commitment and/or strongly resembled box-ticking.[58] Over the longer-term, very frequent changes of national government (see below) – and with it understandings of what precisely needed to be done to fight corruption – also did little to enhance stability in the implementation strategy. This did not stop talk of a second strategy from developing, and by October 2004 a second document ('A program for fighting corruption – An Anti-Corruption Strategy') was published for the 2005–2009 period (a strategy III was also later launched for the period 2011–2015).

These actions did not prompt radical change, but they were the first in a series of steps to try and seriously counteract corrupt practices and cultures. Over this same period party politics in Poland changed quite dramatically, and corruption-issues were some of the major catalysts. Lech Kaczyński, minister for justice and attorney general in the Jerzy Buzek government from June 2000, resigned in July 2001, going on to form the Law and Justice Party (PiS). For Kaczyński and the PiS, corruption 'soon became a central component of their political discourse'.[59] Indeed, by the time of the 2005 election corruption was 'the dominant issue' as parties fought to show they were the most competent in tackling it.[60] Of all the parties, the PiS had the most credibility on this, formed as it was to campaign against corruption and to restore law and order. As Aleks Szczerbiak has noted, the party campaigned to build a 'Fourth Republic', a 'conservative project based on a radical critique of post-1989 Poland as corrupt' that required 'far-reaching moral and political renewal'.[61] The PiS-led government of 2005–2007 subsequently initiated what they claimed was a significant anti-corruption drive.[62]

Lech, and in time his twin brother Jarosław, vowed to root out and destroy Poland's so-called 'grey web' – an alleged behind the scenes network of politicians, influential businessmen, civil servants and underworld figures who, so it was claimed, were carefully, cleverly and secretively controlling the country. In order to blow apart the alleged 'grey web', one of the first things their new government did was to enact a comprehensive civil service reform. The post-2005 reforms of the civil service saw the PiS replace large numbers of civil servants in the ministerial bureaucracy. The logic behind this was that the networks that linked high-level bureaucrats with vested interests would be ripped apart – and this was, in the PiS's reading of the situation, one of the main causes of corruption in Poland. Alongside this managers of state-controlled companies and institutions were also replaced.

In defence of the PiS, they did at least bring a degree of transparency to the politicisation of the process of selecting civil servants – which, so their supporters claim, is a better situation than that which existed previously. As a strategy for seriously combatting corruption, however, critics where not shy in coming forward.[63] The Batory Foundation called them 'particularly dangerous', stressing that the need to be politically neutral was no longer mentioned anywhere in the new legislation and that the list of potentially lucrative senior positions was long (at around 2,000). The discretion of ministers, director generals or leaders of state agencies when choosing these high officials was also greatly enhanced and by 2012 Jan-Hinrik Meyer-Sahling and Tim Veen were claiming that Poland had the joint highest (alongside Slovakia) level of senior civil service politicisation across all of post-communist central and eastern Europe.[64] The chances of 'clientelism or political corruption' were subsequently, according to the Batory Foundation, much increased rather than reduced.[65]

The centrepiece of PiS's anti-corruption drive was, however, the creation of a 'Central Anticorruption Bureau' (CBA) in June 2006. The CBA was given powers enabling it to investigate alleged acts of corruption, to develop ways of preventing corruption and to disseminate anti-corruption information. The PiS clearly hoped that the CBA's significant powers – powers that one influential NGO[66] has described as 'extraordinarily wide-ranging' and even 'excessive' in some cases – would enable it to be a high profile force to rooting out corrupt acts across all government institutions (and beyond), and the government did not shirk from talking the institution's role up.

Yet, the reality quickly proved more complex and the work of the CBA soon became mired in political controversy. Indeed, the very process of creating the CBA highlighted the problems that politicians from across the spectrum had in not just agreeing a specific remit for the organisation, but also in agreeing who should appoint whom, what resources they should have and how broad the scope of their work should be. The PiS's opponents accused the CBA of being a tool of the government, an instrument that the PiS could use to discredit opponents. The first major example of this came when Deputy Prime Minister Andrzej Lepper, an out-spoken and colourful member of Samoobrona, the PiS's coalition partner, was accused of corruption in a number of land deals. This was quickly followed by proposals to investigate members of the opposition Civic Platform Party for (more) apparently dubious land deals – and all this just before the 2007 parliamentary election. The CBA was also involved in activities that looked more like extracts from CSI programmes than serious investigations, the most prominent of which was the arrest – with cameras rolling and the wider world watching – of Miroslaw Garlicki, a well-known surgeon. Suspicions that these actions were more suited to boosting the image of the PiS than to genuinely fighting corruption were widespread, and non-governmental anti-corruption bodies have long called for the CBA to be reorganised in order to remove such suspicions.[67]

Following this flurry of anti-corruption activity in the mid- to late-2000s, enthusiasm for further reform inevitably waned – just as Poland's scores in the WGI and CPI tables started to improve. That this may conceivably have more to do with the inadequacies of the data than the real situation on the ground remains a moot point. As an Ernst and Young report from 2010 noted, 'the novelty of fighting corruption may have worn off, as, perhaps, has the sense of urgency'.[68] Furthermore, attempts to seriously assess the successes and particularly the weaknesses of each of the (three) 'strategies' have always been patchy at best. The PiS's combative approach to tackling corruption may well have made electoral sense, but the party's attempts to monitor the success of the reforms it brought in were much less rigorous than they might have been. Interestingly, this was just as true for successor-administrations as corruption and anti-corruption ceased to grip the public imagination in the way it did in the mid-2000s. Too often citizens found it hard to find information on what impact the anti-corruption strategies were having – if indeed they knew what these strategies were in the first place – and too frequently government announcements were made in arcane language that quickly turned all but the most committed off. This did change through the late 2000s, but 'information deficits' are still real problems.[69]

The lack of a genuinely independent supervisory body overseeing the various tenets of the three anti-corruption strategies also remained a problem. The strategies' long-term effectiveness simply cannot be judged without a body observing and evaluating its work. Different institutions have engaged with the goals of the strategies in different ways, some showing much more sustainable and impressive levels of commitment than others – an oversight body with teeth would be able to pinpoint good and bad practice and point the finger at those who were dragging their feet. It would also be capable of flagging up more general issues of concern as and when they appear. The Batory Foundation has also claimed that some departments simply don't have the resources to deal with all of the demands that the anti-corruption strategies have placed on them. Again, an oversight body would be able to fight departments' corners if their (well-meaning) efforts are simply impractical on account of nothing more than logistical and/or financial weakness.[70]

Post-2009 there has been remarkably little of substance stemming from the government in terms of further developing Poland's anti-corruption framework.[71] The initiatives that have been discussed, and indeed implemented, have either been inconsequential or tantamount to political grandstanding. The most prominent of these was the appointment of a plenipotentiary at the rank of minister to develop approaches aimed to prevent abuses of authority in Poland's public institutions. The creation of this new position sounded like a step forward, but before any real progress could be made the position was abolished, largely on account of insufficient political support as well as an unwillingness to grant the office holder enough resources to genuinely tackle these challenges.[72] Polish society remains quick to condemn corrupt practices, but there is a reluctance to change patterns of behaviour when they bring personal benefits. To be sure, much has changed in Poland over the last 15 years, but the seemingly never-ending flow of scandals illustrates that there is still plenty of room to make progress. Indeed, in August 2012, after a succession of scandals had afflicted ministers in his cabinet, Prime Minister Donald Tusk explicitly stated that he was 'convinced that nepotism is quite prevalent' in Poland and that all of Poland had to try to 'curb the phenomenon'.[73] Tusk was quick to claim that these practices were not limited to one party or indeed to particular sets of institutions, but his general calls to 'build legal rules' to prevent such things from happening will only really prompt changes in behaviour when they are converted into hard, fast and auditable policies.

Lessons from South Korea and Poland

So what can we make of South Korea and Poland's respective attempts at anti-corruption reform? As indicated in the introduction to this chapter, we are looking for evidence of progress in four discrete areas; the ability to sharpen up democratic oversight procedures, increased accountability of actions of ministers and high-ranking civil servants, evidence of progress in increasing the transparency of relationships between business elites and political elites and finally assisting the media and other investigatory authorities in analysing alleged corrupt behaviour.[74]

Both countries have made progress, although false steps appear almost as common as forward ones. Politicians in both countries have, in their own ways, looked to implement similar anti-corruption mechanisms – with at times quite different results. Both looked to introduce a high profile anti-corruption agency to oversee general anti-corruption activity. The Polish CBA started off controversially and was widely criticised as being a tool of the then governing party, but slowly it has developed in to an organisation that has been able to make at least a partial impact. The story in South Korea is altogether different, and by the time the ACA there was merged with other bodies in 2008 it had long since ceased to be a genuine force for change. The Polish CBA was able to impose itself, it was able to ask awkward questions – that it did not do so to everyone's liking is not the point, it did at least begin to shake things up. Despite all its imperfections, the experience of the Polish CBA may well be one worth studying by anti-corruption thinkers elsewhere.

Where South Korea has done rather more impressively than Poland is in the realm of civil society. Polish civil society condemns corruption, but it has been depressingly inactive in genuinely moving against it. In South Korea, meanwhile, a significant number of anti-corruption NGOs have engaged with policy-makers to try and change the political environment. They have pushed for the increased accountability of ministers and they have aggressively called for more transparency in business links with politics. They have clearly not been completely successful, but the murky world of chaebol dominance is now at least a little less murky than it once was. The fourth of our points to look for, strengthening the powers of those investigating corruption, has, albeit indirectly, occurred, as the almost never-ending reporting of scandals and allegedly inappropriate behaviour illustrates.

Developing meaningful anti-corruption strategies in Poland and South Korea has been a messy undertaking. At times political will has appeared to be there, at other times it has looked alarmingly like business as usual if under a different guise. This is reflected in the patchy governance data as well as in popular perceptions of how successful South Korean and Polish politicians have been in tackling corruption. That there is a whole lot more to be done is certainly beyond doubt.

5
Germany and the UK: The Slow and Winding Road to Reform

Introduction

Both Germany and the UK have traditionally been viewed as countries where corruption is largely under control.[1] Corruption was never taken to be non-existent or irrelevant, but it was, for much of the post-war period, seen as something that happened largely as bad applies enriched themselves but where systems of oversight, compliance and cultures of 'doing the right thing' would ultimately prevail. Indeed, these attitudes were not just evident in Germany and the UK, they prevailed across much of the western world.

Only in the 1980s – and arguably later than that in some quarters – did this slowly begin to change. Germany was rocked by, amongst other things, the Flick Affair, an episode that enveloped much of the political class, whilst through the 1990s the UK was swamped by a whole series of stories of under the rubrics of 'sleaze' and 'scandal'.[2] Indeed, at times public life seemed to be plagued by a litany of high profile misdemeanours, ranging from a (German) chancellor maintaining a whole system of illegal bank accounts purely to side-track the country's laws on party funding to a British Prime Minister claiming that his government, and indeed public officials more generally, needed to (infamously) go 'back to basics' in order to weed out inappropriate behaviour.[3] Legions of other 'scandalous' events unfolded both before and after these two particular episodes, as in little more than a decade perceptions of corruption in both the UK and Germany changed considerably.

But we should be careful before equating a rise in the number of scandals with a rise in the number and extent of corrupt acts actually taking place. Furthermore, we should also be just a touch careful before concluding that there has been a failure of implementation, or indeed a lack of will, in terms of the proposed anti-corruption policies and strategies that have materialised on the back of this alleged dip (or dive bomb, if you believe some) in public standards. Scandals have existed for as long as representative politics has, but coverage of them has changed remarkably in the last quarter century.[4] The rise of the 24/7 media certainly ensures that more scandalous acts are reported, but this is not necessarily evidence that more of them are taking place. Furthermore, it may well say nothing at all about wider issues of corruption and anti-corruption, and this is something that often gets lost in the sound of uproar that periodically curses through the popular press.

Given that, the cases of the UK and Germany are interesting for a number of reasons. They are both advanced, industrial economies with embedded democratic structures. They have comparatively unpoliticised civil services and both have parliamentary systems where there is a close connection between a parliamentary majority and the executive. They possess free and vibrant media landscapes and politicians in both countries have, until recently, largely believed corruption to be a problem that other states had. That has changed in both countries in recent times, hence we should see some evidence of governments trying to 'sharpen up' their respective anti-corruption acts.

The WGI data in Tables 5.1 and 5.2 shows us how the two states were performing in terms of governance quality between the mid-1990s and early 2000s. As is to be expected, both states perform well across the board. Germany is particularly strong in terms of 'rule of law' (top ten percentile across all four points in time and that with the lowest standard error scores of any of the six indicators) and 'control of corruption' (where it is again easily in the top percentile, with truly outstanding scores in 1996 and 1998). The CPI data in Table 5.5 is paradoxically less impressive, but this is likely to be as it is less accurate than the WGI scores. Germany consistently polled around 8.0 in terms of CPI scores, the only exceptions being 2001 and 2002 when it registered 7.4 and 7.3. That this happens just after revelations not just about former chancellor Helmut Kohl's illegal bank accounts but also a series of other illegal party funding issues probably pulls the scores down. That there was more corruption in

Table 5.1   The quality of governance in Germany, 1996–2002

Governance Indicator	Sources	Year	Percentile Rank (0–100)	Governance Score (–2.5 – +2.5)	Standard Error
Voice and	8	2002	94.7	+1.41	0.20
Accountability	7	2000	89.9	+1.32	0.22
	6	1998	88.9	+1.29	0.23
	6	1996	90.4	+1.33	0.22
Political	6	2002	83.7	+1.02	0.28
Stability	5	2000	95.2	+1.32	0.30
	4	1998	89.4	+1.17	0.34
	4	1996	88.9	+1.21	0.36
Government	5	2002	92.2	+1.72	0.19
Effectiveness	5	2000	94.1	+1.91	0.21
	5	1998	95.1	+1.93	0.21
	5	1996	93.7	+1.84	0.23
Regulatory	6	2002	92.6	+1.54	0.23
Quality	6	2000	91.7	+1.47	0.23
	6	1998	87.7	+1.22	0.27
	6	1996	91.2	+1.38	0.27
Rule of Law	8	2002	93.8	+1.61	0.18
	8	2000	93.8	+1.59	0.16
	7	1998	93.8	+1.61	0.19
	7	1996	93.8	+1.57	0.19
Control of	5	2002	93.7	+2.01	0.18
Corruption	5	2000	93.2	+1.90	0.23
	5	1998	95.1	+2.16	0.19
	5	1996	94.6	+1.99	0.23

Source: http://info.worldbank.org/governance/wgi/sc_chart.asp# viewed on 15th August 2012

Germany then than at any other point in the time period analysed here is anything other than clear. The WGI data, meanwhile, does show a degree of nuance, with the country's 'political stability' scores showing a fair degree of variance across the six year period. That

Table 5.2   The quality of governance in the UK, 1996–2002

Governance Indicator	Sources	Year	Percentile Rank (0–100)	Governance Score (–2.5 – +2.5)	Standard Error
Voice and	8	2002	89.9	+1.27	0.20
Accountability	7	2000	90.9	+1.34	0.22
	6	1998	87.5	+1.19	0.23
	6	1996	88.5	+1.29	0.22
Political	6	2002	65.4	+0.61	0.28
Stability	5	2000	79.3	+0.99	0.30
	4	1998	77.4	+0.88	0.34
	4	1996	76.9	+0.92	0.36
Government	5	2002	93.2	+1.85	0.19
Effectiveness	5	2000	93.7	+1.86	0.21
	5	1998	94.6	+1.92	0.21
	5	1996	95.1	+1.88	0.23
Regulatory	6	2002	96.6	+1.74	0.23
Quality	6	2000	98.0	+1.85	0.23
	6	1998	99.0	+2.01	0.27
	6	1996	99.5	+2.02	0.27
Rule of Law	8	2002	94.3	+1.64	0.18
	8	2000	94.3	+1.65	0.16
	7	1998	95.2	+1.74	0.19
	7	1996	94.7	+1.59	0.19
Control of	5	2002	95.6	+2.13	0.18
Corruption	5	2000	96.1	+2.24	0.23
	5	1998	96.6	+2.23	0.19
	5	1996	96.1	+2.12	0.23

Source: http://info.worldbank.org/governance/wgi/sc_chart.asp# viewed on 15th August 2012

having been said, the German scores match more or less any country in the world in terms of good quality governance.

The same can generally be said for the UK, where all quality of governance indicators are good. The UK's 'control of corruption' scores are particularly impressive, with a low of +2.12 and a high of +2.24; the allegedly sleazy years under John Major's tutelage did not apparently do much to damage the UK's ability to combat corruption. This is backed up by data in Table 5.6, illustrating that until the late 2000s the UK performed well in the CPI, with scores regularly above 8.5. A parliamentary expenses scandal (see below) may well have been the catalyst for a dip in CPI scores, even if the actual level of corruption in the UK is unlikely to have changed simply on account of parliamentarians being revealed as manipulating the expenses system. In other words, it is likely that this high profile scandal has had a disproportionate effect on Britain's CPI scores.

If 'control of corruption' is a highpoint for the UK, 'political stability' scores would appear to be the weak spot. Scores there diverge from those of the other five indicators by a considerable margin, indicating that uncertainties in the political arena are tangible. Whilst the UK clearly was not on the verge of lurching into unseemly conflict with itself, WGI data does indicate that under the first Blair administration there were problems in this area. This may appear to be surprising, but the phenomenon of states with otherwise strong governance scores elsewhere scoring poorly here is actually more common than one might expect. This is as this indicator 'captures perceptions of the likelihood of politically motivated violence' and, importantly, this includes terrorism.[5] The post-9/11 USA, for example, has scored noticeably worse than it did pre-9/11, just as the UK's close relationship with the USA saw its scores suffer on account of the perceived increase in salience of a potential terrorist attack (which did indeed become a genuine attack in July 2005). As an aside, it is therefore important to remember that lower scores are not necessarily endogenous to governance – external events and challenges can and do impact on them.

Be that as it may, this should not distract from strong scores in both 'government effectiveness' and 'regulatory quality', as well as consistent performances in terms of 'rule of law'. The picture in the UK is therefore similar to that in Germany, with the only real outlier being that of 'political stability'.

If we look at the WGI control of corruption data for the extended period from 1996 to 2010, then we see an impressive picture of consistency in both countries. In Germany (Table 5.3), the high

Table 5.3   **Control of corruption, Germany, 1996–2010**

Country	Sources	Year	Percentile Rank (0–100)	Governance Score (−2.5 − +2.5)	Standard Error
Germany	13	2010	93.3	+1.70	0.19
	12	2009	92.3	+1.70	0.18
	12	2008	92.7	+1.73	0.17
	12	2007	92.2	+1.70	0.17
	11	2006	92.7	+1.79	0.16
	9	2005	93.7	+1.87	0.18
	9	2004	93.2	+1.86	0.18
	7	2003	93.7	+1.94	0.20
	6	2002	93.7	+2.01	0.18
	6	2000	93.2	+1.90	0.23
	4	1998	95.1	+2.16	0.19
	3	1996	94.6	+1.99	0.23

Source: WGI data, accessed 15th August 2012

point was reached in 1998 (2.16), but even though the scores have slipped since, the country has nonetheless remained in the top percentile rank. That having been said, Germany's governance scores have fallen rather more acutely than that ranking would perhaps indicate, with the governance scores of 2007–2010 around 1.7 – a reasonable distance away from scores achieved in the 1996–2002 era. Over time, something appears to have slipped, even if we cannot from this data tell precisely what.

The data for the UK shows a similar pattern to that of Germany. The UK's figures are much stronger around the time of the millennium than they are at the end of the first decade of the 21st century, and whilst the slippage is not dramatic, it certainly remains noticeable. Indeed, the UK's performance from 1996–2005 was year in, year out stronger than that of Germany, but by 2010 the UK had slipped behind the Federal Republic. This chapter will shed at least some light on why that has been the case.

Given the governance data as it is outlined here, this leaves policy-makers in Germany and the UK with an altogether different set of challenges to those analysed thus far. As was discussed in Chapter 2, governance regimes where corruption is relatively low

Table 5.4   Control of corruption, UK, 1996–2010

Country	Sources	Year	Percentile Rank (0–100)	Governance Score (–2.5 – +2.5)	Standard Error
UK	8	2010	90.0	+1.48	0.19
	8	2009	91.4	+1.54	0.18
	8	2008	92.2	+1.67	0.17
	8	2007	92.7	+1.72	0.17
	8	2006	93.2	+1.79	0.16
	6	2005	94.6	+1.90	0.18
	6	2004	94.6	+1.96	0.18
	5	2003	95.1	+2.07	0.20
	5	2002	95.6	+2.13	0.18
	5	2000	96.1	+2.24	0.23
	5	1998	96.6	+2.23	0.19
	5	1996	96.1	+2.12	0.23

Source: WGI data, accessed 15th August 2012

and governance quality is high are likely to need to do a number of things.

- Use the strong legal systems, high standards of regulatory quality and the strong cultures of voice and accountability to bring in, or beef up, independent anti-corruption agencies.
- With levels of accountability generally high, it is likely that emphasis will need to be placed on the specifics of financial accountability. New laws, rules and regulations to clarify codes of practices are likely to be necessary.
- Increase awareness of good and bad practice and of what is and isn't morally acceptable behaviour in public office.
- Strive to prosecute those at all ends – but particularly the top – of the spectrum who are caught behaving in a corrupt fashion.

All of these initiatives have been discussed in some way, shape or form in Germany and the UK. Some died a relatively quick death, whereas others have become subjects of genuine public interest (such as, for example, the UK Bribery Act that was passed in 2010). The remainder of this chapter analyses the initiatives that have appeared in more detail.

Tackling corruption in Germany

Until relatively recently, corruption in the domestic context was not something that Germans spent too much time thinking about. There were, of course, exceptions but generally corruption was perceived to happen in other places and to be caused by other people.[6] This prompted one of Germany's most-well respected analysts of corruption, Ulrich von Alemann, to note that the 'notion of corruption' was an 'almost unknown term' in domestic political analysis.[7] The Germans, to be fair, were not alone in taking this view about their own politics, as across western Europe serious empirical analysis of corruption in Europe remained noticeable by its absence. Such thinking prompted Theodor Eschenburg to claim in 1970 that the German people had been 'spoiled by an extremely honest public administration', and were subsequently very sensitive to administrative malpractice.[8] The lack of perceived corruption was, according to Eschenburg, important in helping Germans remain particularly sensitive to situations where 'black sheep' might appear to abuse the country's system of good governance. A decade and a half later, and this approach appeared to be very much intact, as was exemplified by another leading light of German political science, Paul Noack, when he claimed that Germans continued to believe that 'theirs is one of those nations that has proved to be most resistant to corruption'.[9]

Those times of complacency bordering on arrogance are now long since gone. It is easy to assume that the Flick Scandal was the key moment when everything began to change, but in truth a steady trickle of cases – at both national and local level – saw the myth of a natural German (and European) superiority implode. Yet, awareness of corruption took a long time to filter into legal and procedural changes, and until 1999 it was, for example, perfectly legal in Germany to bribe foreign officials to gain contracts. Furthermore, these bribes were even tax deductible.[10] And German business did not appear to be aware of the need to adopt ethically sound practices until even later than then, as particularly high profile scandals at Volkswagen (2005) and Siemens (2006) illustrated.[11] These were by no means the only ones.

By the turn of the 21st century German attitudes had moved full circle, becoming highly critical of their public servants, as many

Table 5.5   Germany's performance in Transparency International's Corruption Perceptions Index, 1998–2011

Year	Score	Rank
1998	7.9	15 (out of 85)
1999	8.0	14 (out of 99)
2000	7.6	17 (out of 90)
2001	7.4	20 (out of 91)
2002	7.3	18 (out of 102)
2003	7.7	16 (out of 133)
2004	8.2	15 (out of 146)
2005	8.2	16 (out of 159)
2006	8.0	16 (out of 163)
2007	7.8	16 (out of 180)
2008	7.9	14 (out of 180)
2009	8.0	14 (out of 180)
2010	7.9	15 (out of 178)
2011	8.0	14 (out of 183)

Source: Transparency International's website

were criticised of being in politics to enrich themselves at the expense of the masses. Indeed, the increasing number of scandals in German public life led to a whole new vocabulary developing, as Germans complained firstly of 'Parteienverdrossenheit' (disillusionment with political parties), then 'Politikverdrossenheit' (disillusionment with politics) but finally, and most worrying of all, 'Politikverachtung' (a disdain for politics).

This doom and gloom is, however, tilting the balance too far the other way. According to Transparency International's most recent (2012) National Integrity System Report, the Federal Republic does still come 'at the top end of the NIS assessment system' and scores very well across 'all analysed areas and government levels'.[12] Indeed, TI further added that Germany has a 'very good integrity system' that is well equipped 'for preventing and repressing corruption'.[13] Recent governments have therefore been acting within the confines of a democratic, legal, institutional and economic system that is generally seen to work well and to be well suited to dealing with corruption challenges.

It is perhaps worth remembering this when looking at the specific activities of German governments, mainly as the bulk of the most recent anti-corruption activity came well over a decade ago, in the mid-late 1990s.[14] The measures that are currently in place remain highly diverse, although they centre around the 'Concept of Corruption Prevention' developed by the Standing Conference of Federal State Ministers and Senators of the Interior (IMK) held in May 1995.[15] A number of specific anti-corruption initiatives have been put forward in subsequent years, the most prominent of which was the 1998 Anti-Corruption Act. Interestingly the 1998 act remains the last to be implemented without clearly discernible external influence, indicating the reactive nature of policy-making in this area. Other pieces of legislation have certainly followed (in 1999, for example, the Act Against International Corruption and the EU Anti-Corruption Acts were both passed, whilst further amendments were made to bribery laws in 2002), but they have all, for better or worse, 'originated in international legal instruments'.[16] Be that as it may, these new laws 'greatly expanded Germany's anti-corruption focus' and signalled a step change in how corruption was viewed.[17]

Critics claim that the apparent need for external impetus before anything substantive changes shows that German law makers remain dismissive of the need to seriously overhaul the country's anti-corruption infrastructure. They further point out that Germany has a tendency to implement just the minimum requirements when meeting the international obligations it signs up to.[18] Indeed, sometimes Germany does not even meet those; Germany has not ratified the UN Convention against Corruption (at the time of writing 161 countries had) – and this despite significant pressure from German business to do so – as well as two Council of Europe anti-corruption conventions.[19] There also seems little likelihood that it plans to sign on the dotted line any time in the near future.[20] Germany has also failed to adopt a number of the specific anti-corruption measures recommended to it by the Council of Europe and OECD.[21]

To be fair to German policy-makers, German criticisms of the UNCAC in particular are more procedural than substantive, and conservative parliamentarians in particular have been unwilling to sign it for reasons that are specific to the German case. German Members of Parliament are, for example, not civil servants, yet some policy-makers claim that if the treaty were ratified then they would de facto become so – something that, in the German case, would have complicated and convoluted ramifications. A new 'Members of the Federal Parliament Act' was also passed in 2005, and this at around the same time that the Members Code of Conduct was being updated – both of which compelled parliamentarians to be more open about their secondary earnings and commitments than they ever had been before. Critics still claim that laws pertaining to the corruption of parliamentarians remain both narrowly defined and have only a 'very small scope for practical application', but this shouldn't distract from the fact that the laws have been tightened up.[22] Even Transparency International has subsequently been prepared to admit that the statutory provisions that 'safeguard the independence, transparency and integrity of the legislature and the Members of the Bundestag respectively, are comprehensive'.[23] Whilst this is still unlikely to placate all, Germany's long-standing commitment to anti-corruption agencies such as the Group of States Against Corruption (GRECO) as well as the OECD, plus a plethora of other international organisations that have anti-corruption initiatives indicates the fact that UNCAC has not (yet) been ratified should not render Germany's anti-corruption efforts null and void.

And yet Gerhard Schröder's centre-left government (1998–2005), Angela Merkel's 'Grand Coalition' (2005–2009) and her centre-right government (since 2009) have hardly trail blazed in terms of prioritising anti-corruption initiatives. The Ministry of Justice did draft a second Anti-Corruption Act (*Zweites Gesetz zur Bekämpfung der Korruption*) in 2006, with the stated intention of factoring new international agreements into Germany's criminal code. Ultimately, the draft got nowhere near the statute book, and that mainly as there was, and is, no consensus that Germany's first anti-corruption law actually needs radically changing. As Nick Lord persuasively argues, a significant number of German policy-makers remain confident that 'national provisions on corruption-related criminal offences' are already located in existing legal statutes and there is therefore little reason to set out on wholesale changes.[24]

And it is in the nature of Germany's highly legalistic approach to public life that we find the reasons for much of the divergence away from the four key anti-corruption points that we outlined at the beginning of this chapter. The instincts of many German policy-makers are to ask whether their 'hard measures' (which come mostly in the form of laws) are sufficient in doing the job of tackling corruption. If they are not, then the initial assumption is that laws will have to be tightened up (or better ones thought up), whether the aim is to make legal enforcement more efficient and effective or to maintain high moral and ethical standards of behaviour.[25] It is precisely this that led Sebastian Wolf to bemoan the Bundestag's 'piecemeal approach of implementing only minimum requirements by means of auxiliary laws' when it had, for example, the opportunity to integrate both the 1999 'Act Against International Corruption' and the 2002 'EU Anti-Corruption Act' into the pre-existing criminal code.[26] The 'soft measures' – such as codes of ethics or principled declarations – are traditionally seen as playing a more symbolic role, with the aim of 'raising consciousness, demonstrat[ing] commitment and promot[ing] trust', and it is here that German policy-makers have lagged behind countries such as the USA and particularly the UK (see below).[27]

In other words, German politicians are much more likely to choose legal solutions to corruption problems as they tend to fit in with their 'inherited cognitive patterns' and 'existing institutional structures' than are British ones. Germany's Roman Law tradition is a recipe for institutional conservatism, whereas in countries like the UK – marked as it is by a Common Law tradition – there will be a greater tendency to go for pragmatic solutions, and to downplay the systematic thinking that characterises the German *Rechtstaat*. This is not to say that change will not happen and adaptation is impossible – clearly it is not, and the 'existing tool-kit can be enlarged or altered and the salience of new measures be enhanced by promotional activities of interested actors, in particular by international organisations'.[28] But we should not be surprised that Britain has been lighter on its feet than Germany in this regard.

The one area where Germany is highly unlikely to move is that of a specialised anti-corruption agency. Germany has developed an anti-corruption ethos that tends to see prevention as being the job of the various supervisory bodies whereas repression is solely for the law enforcement agencies.[29] Crafting a remit for an ACA in this culture would be problematic. There is subsequently no popular support for an ACA. Furthermore, Germany's federal structure ensures that setting up an over-arching anti-corruption unit with executive powers would also prove difficult. There would either need to be far-reaching and genuinely ground-breaking changes to the distribution of powers between the national and *Land* (regional) levels or an ACA would find itself faced with a myriad of overlapping competencies. The first eventuality is unrealistic, whilst the second is unwelcome, and any move to create an ACA in the form that has been done elsewhere would subsequently cause much more trouble and confusion than it would be worth – and this even though both the UNCAC and the Council of Europe's Criminal Law Convention on Corruption both recommend precisely that.[30]

There has, on the other hand, been a move to prosecute more of those caught behaving in a corrupt fashion. Both Volkswagen and Siemens saw high-ranking officials sent to prison for their roles in the corrupt practices that those companies had indulged in, whilst both Siemens and BASF (after it was caught fixing prices) paid fines totalling over a billion (Siemens) and half a billion (BASF) dollars. Prosecutions for corruption in the German business world more generally have, in the words of the New York Times, 'soared' and in 2011 the OECD praised Germany for the fact that 70 individuals and six companies had been successfully prosecuted over the previous six years.[31] Germany's increasing willingness to prosecute business leaders who indulge in bribery in particular has subsequently led to a real change of tone and in 2012 Markus Funk and Jess Dance bluntly advised 'companies doing business in Germany or with German companies' to make themselves very 'familiar with Germany's anticorruption laws'.[32] A significant number – and certainly more than ever before – of both politicians and civil servants have also come into the firing line.[33]

Tackling corruption in the UK

UK politicians, much like those in Germany, traditionally spent much more time talking about corruption in other places than they did corruption at home. Even as late as 1997, Andrew Adonis (soon to become a Labour peer and government minister) observed that Britain 'is widely seen as the model of the non-corrupt industrial democracy'. For good measure, he also added that 'it certainly sees itself that way'.[34] However, over the last 20 years (and particularly within the last decade) there have been serious attempts made to increase the effectiveness of Britain's anti-corruption institutions and also to sharpen the legal position within which allegedly corrupt

Table 5.6   The UK's performance in Transparency International's Corruption Perceptions Index, 1998–2011

Year	Score	Rank
1998	8.7	11 (out of 85)
1999	8.6	13 (out of 99)
2000	8.7	10 (out of 90)
2001	8.3	13 (out of 91)
2002	8.7	10 (out of 102)
2003	8.7	11 (out of 133)
2004	8.6	11 (out of 146)
2005	8.6	11 (out of 159)
2006	8.6	11 (out of 163)
2007	8.4	12 (out of 180)
2008	7.7	16 (out of 180)
2009	7.7	17 (out of 180)
2010	7.6	20 (out of 178)
2011	7.8	16 (out of 183)

Source: Transparency International's website

acts can be prosecuted. That actually changing things has at times taken a long time should not detract from the fact that the UK has, at the very least, made concerted efforts to tackle its corruption problems – and this even though its CPI scores have recently been going down and not up!

Even if the UK 'does not have a serious problem with traditional forms of corruption', it became clear in the 1990s that the existing institutional framework certainly needed an overhaul.[35] Dawn Oliver even goes as far as to put a (more or less) exact date on when 'a problem of real corruption' was 'recognised to exist' in the UK – 'about 1995'.[36] As scandal after scandal began to envelop Prime Minister John Major's two administrations (1990–1997) Oliver was not alone in feeling that the moral and ethical standards of those in power in the UK were not what they should be.[37] And, John Major – never during his time as PM accused of indiscretions of the type that some of his ministers and backbenchers were, although it did later transpire that he had a four year extra-marital affair with one of his own junior ministers – evidently agreed that there was a problem, setting up the 'Committee on Standards in Public Life' in November 1994. This followed the high profile Cash for Questions scandal as well as a number of highly embarrassing episodes that can be analysed under the rubric of 'Back to Basics', a request that Major made at the Conservatives' annual conference in October 1993 when he called for a return to more old fashioned family values.[38]

The Committee on Standards in Public Life, or Nolan Committee (named after its first chairman, Lord Nolan), was tasked to 'inquire in to public life more generally' rather than 'investigate individual cases', with the aim of 'embody[ing] a new world of self-regulation and tightening of the rules governing the conduct of people in public life'.[39] It was placed 'at the apex of a large and growing set of bureaucracies' with the aim of 'regulating the conduct of public servants in all spheres of public life'.[40] And, as and when the time came, the Nolan Committee's first report did not pull any punches.[41] Although Nolan felt unable to comment on whether standards in public life had notably worsened over time and he remained convinced that the vast majority of public servants behaved admirably, the committee nonetheless claimed that there were 'weaknesses in the procedures for maintaining and enforcing those standards'. The report carried on to note that 'people in public life are not always as clear as they should be about where the boundaries of acceptable conduct lie' and that this 'calls for urgent remedial action'.[42] The Committee on Standards in Public Life was not empowered to change the rules, but its conclusions certainly criticised the political class in a way that they had rarely had to endure in the past. Indeed, the majority of its recommendations were implemented within months of the report being published, as a new 'Select Committee on Standards and Privileges' took over looking into MPs' interests and a parliamentary commissioner for standards was brought in.

The effects of the tumultuous Major years were, however, largely superficial. And for two specific reasons. Firstly, Tony Blair's electoral triumph in 1997 was seen as the beginning of a new era in British politics, one hopefully free of the sleazy underbelly that had come to characterise the final years of Tory rule. Whilst Labour under Blair largely (although not completely) avoided some of the more sordid sexual scandals that had beset the Tories, it did not take long before 'New' Labour was having corruption-related problems of its own, whether it be in the form of electoral fraud, 'cash for access' to ministers, controversial party donations by sporting magnates or more general accusations of 'spinning' the political agenda.[43] Labour parliamentarians were, so it appeared, just as able to commit indiscretions as were the Tories. Secondly, on closer inspection it also became clear that the cultural change that the Committee on Standards in Public Life was supposed to herald had not happened. A framework of soft ethics regulation now existed, and public servants certainly paid lip service to it, but the unfortunate case of Elizabeth Filkin, appointed Parliamentary Commissioner for Standards (PCS) in 1999, illustrated that if independent oversight was going to lead to tougher questions being asked about the behaviour of parliamentarians, then it was not welcome. Filkin upheld complaints against a number of high profile government members concerning their external interests, and, impressively diligent though she was, she inevitably began to make enemies.[44] As her term came to an end she was not simply re-appointed, but rather told she would have to re-apply for her own job. She refused and ultimately opted to stand down.[45]

The significance of this was not immediately apparent, and it took the onset of another round of scandals in 2009 to really hammer home how important it was to behave in morally and ethically sound ways. The first Blair government had passed a not uncontroversial Freedom of Information Act (FOI) in 2000, granting citizens access to public records held on them. In 2000 no one considered using an FOI request to get hold of information on the expenses that parliamentarians claimed, but by the middle of the decade FOI campaigners, and particularly Heather Brooke, were campaigning vigorously to see the details of all these transactions. Despite the attempts of the House of Commons authorities in general, and the Speaker of the House in particular, to thwart them, they were ultimately successful – leading to the parliamentary expenses episode of 2009.[46] This episode shook Westminster, and the whole political class, to its core, as hundreds of parliamentarians found themselves defending their (what at times appeared to be) outlandish expenses claims. That 'flipping' houses and claiming mortgage tax relief, not to mention getting the tax payer to clean your moat or build a nice house for your ducks in the middle of your pond, was within the rules was not the point. To many people, parliamentarians appeared to have got into the lazy habit of making the most out of a generous expenses regime, whilst never being shy of asking others to scrimp and save to ensure that the nation's books balanced.[47] The impression that this episode left was one of a British political class paying lip service to the need to maintain ethical standards whilst themselves behaving in a way that the vast majority of citizens felt was essentially corrupt.[48] Or, as TI more diplomatically put it, there were a significant number 'of integrity and accountability mechanisms in Parliament, but these have not worked very well in practice'.[49]

Out of touch though politicians certainly looked during the parliamentary expenses episode, moves had actually been afoot long before then to sharpen up the UK's anti-corruption infrastructure. And with good reason. As the UK entered the 21st century even the then Lord Chancellor, Lord Falconer, argued that the body of law in this area was 'complex, inconsistent and outdated' whilst former Home Secretary, Jack Straw, described the legislation as 'old and anachronistic'.[50] Furthermore, Paul Heywood points out that there were at least 15 different bodies that could plausibly be understood as 'ethical watchdogs', and that is not including the separate arrangements that apply to Wales and Scotland.[51] Depending on your point of view, Britain's regulatory landscape was subsequently a 'patchwork quilt', a 'multi-piece jigsaw' or a 'game of chess'.[52] What it certainly was not was streamlined and easy for the outsider to make sense of.

For much of the 20th century the core of the UK's anti-corruption legislation compromised three acts; the 1889 Public Bodies Corrupt Practices Act, the 1906 Prevention of Corruption Act and the 1916 Prevention of Corruption Act. The 2001 Anti-Terrorism, Crime and Security Act added more depth to this, including as it did a number of clauses on overseas corruption, whilst there are a number of other laws that ostensibly look to do other things but also have a corruption element to them (the 1925 Honours (Prevention of Abuses) Act being one such example).[53] Through the 2000s the Labour government did not shirk from trying to update this rather hotchpotch of a picture, and a great deal of time and effort was spent in trying to both update and consolidate anti-corruption legislation.[54] This led to the passing of a UK Fraud Act in 2006 and ultimately to the UK Bribery Act (UKBA) of 2010.

The scope and extent of the territory covered in the UKBA renders it a 'groundbreaking' piece of legislation that put the UK 'in the forefront of the struggle against international corruption'.[55] Private bribery is now criminalised in the UK, whilst companies are now required to maintain levels of transparency that were previously unheard of. The UKBA even takes on the particularly thorny area of facilitation payments, or 'small bribes paid to facilitate routine government action',[56] bluntly condemning them as wrong and not allowing any exemptions for them.[57] It also criminalises 'the failure to have adequate procedures to prevent bribery', compelling companies to actively take measures to eradicate the risk of being drawn into potentially corrupt activity.[58] Ultimately, the effect of the act will of course hinge on the ability of the Serious Fraud Office to secure convictions. Be that as it may, there have perhaps inevitably been warnings from some quarters about the allegedly draconian nature of some its provisions; whilst some journalists were quick to sensationalise the story (particularly in terms of some of the limits placed on corporate hospitality[59]), there were genuine worries about UK businesses now being put at a disadvantage when compared with their international competitors.[60] Conversely, there have been others (most notably Transparency International) who have argued that some of the official guidance that has been published alongside the UKBA came dangerously close to helping businesses get around some of the UKBA's provisions. Non-UK companies listed on the London Stock Exchange, for example, are not automatically covered by the UKBA and UK companies can, if they are that way inclined, effectively 'outsource' bribery by 'building a chain of subcontractors sufficiently long to distance itself from bribe paying'.[61] Only time will tell whether any of these fears are well-founded, but one thing is clear – the act undoubtedly marks a step change in UK anti-corruption legislation.

The UK has subsequently made considerable progress over the last 15 years. TI points out that there has been 'considerable improvements' made to the UK's National Integrity System in general and also to 'anti-corruption activity' more specifically.[62] Anti-corruption agencies talk to each other rather more, whilst anti-corruption legislation has undoubtedly been streamlined and updated. However, there are still worries over resources, a lack of leadership and the transparency of the process, not to mention the abnormally large number of agencies with investigative capacity to look into cases of corruption. Alongside the law enforcement agencies (regional police forces, the Serious Organised Crime Agency, HM Revenue and Customs and the UK Border Agency) there are also government departments with internal investigative capacity (DWP, NHS, HM Prison Service, MoD and DEFRA) as well as and other non-departmental public bodies (the Charity Commission; Standards for England). Add to this organisations such as the Audit Commission (that has conducted major corruption investigations into local authorities in Westminster and Doncaster) and it is clear that joined-up anti-corruption work is going to be a challenge.[63]

The closest that the UK comes to a conventional anti-corruption agency is the Serious Fraud Office (SFO), working alongside the Overseas Anti-Corruption Unit (OACU). These organisations have managed to achieve some high-profile successes, but their task is not a straightforward one.[64] Tackling corruption is only one (significant, but not predominant) part of the SFO's workload, generally accounting for around a third of its budget. The OACU, meanwhile, also has to exist in an institutional environment where fighting corruption is only one part of the remit. There is also a worry that the extra activities the SFO is now required to do will stretch its limited resources further. The fact that these resources have been cut – from £39.5m in 2010–2011 to £30.5m by 2014–2015 – in the recent rounds of spending cuts will not help.[65] This is even more apparent given that the SFO claims to be pursuing a 'zero-tolerance' policy in its investigations.[66] Given this, TI is particularly scathing about the effect that the wide-ranging cuts imposed by the post-2010 Conservative-Liberal Democrat government are having on anti-corruption in general, emphasising that the loss in capacity will 'directly and (almost certainly) negatively impact upon the UK National Integrity System'. Furthermore, the government could not even explain how, for example, the abolition of the Audit Commission was actually going to save any money, whilst the Decentralisation and Localism Bill looks set to 'dismantle the entire local government integrity framework, including the statutory code of conduct, replacing it with whatever voluntary arrangements local authorities choose, or can afford'.[67] This does not bode well for the future.

The rather dismal case of BAE in 2006 – when an inquiry into BAE Systems' $43bn al-Yamamah arms deal with Saudi Arabia was dropped after Prime Minister Tony Blair intervened in the case – also illustrated that transparency and a respect for due process are not always forthcoming.[68] The fact that the BAE settlement took 11 months to reach the public domain – and even then not all information was forthcoming – is a further illustration of the challenges that anti-corruption campaigners can face. Indeed, cases like this do much to set back efforts to increase public trust in public officials' ability to fight corrupt practices.

Lessons from Germany and the UK

Germany and the UK are in qualitatively different positions to the states that were analysed in Chapters 3 and 4. Although clearly not perfect, they have strong sets of anti-corruption institutions and cultures that are not, as a rule, conducive to corrupt activity. That corruption still exists is beyond question, but the challenges are more nuanced and particular than those that governments in many parts of the world face.

The literature indicates that Germany and the UK should subsequently look to develop their anti-corruption agendas in four specific areas (see page 99). Both countries have used their well-developed legal systems and their independent judiciaries to nuance their legal frameworks. The British attempts have been more radical than the German ones, but neither country has opted to introduce an anti-corruption agency. In Germany's case this would pose major institutional and cultural challenges, and it has subsequently never been a topic for public discussion. In the UK, meanwhile, the case for such an agency is stronger, but UK elites have preferred to work within the current framework to empower organisations such as the SFO and to beef up the current legal framework (by introducing laws such as the UKBA). There is therefore plenty of evidence here to suggest that ACAs, despite theoretical support, are unlikely to be popular choices in terms of supplementing anti-corruption frameworks in states with good quality governance.

Germany has been much more proactive in fulfilling the second set of goals outlined on page 99 concerning financial accountability. The high profile scandals around companies such as Siemens and BASF have prompted German prosecutors to be much more combative in making the already existing set of anti-corruption laws work. Courts appear much more willing to send high-profile executives to prison and to impose significant fines, contributing to a real feeling that the business culture in Germany is finally changing. The UK authorities have tried to make progress here, but as yet the effects are much less discernible. It is plausible that with the 2010 UKBA this will change – the framework is certainly there for it to do so – but British prosecutors are not yet as able as their German counterparts to secure prosecutions.

The steady stream of scandals in both countries has led public servants in both countries to review their own moral and ethical behaviour. Until the late 2000s the results of this apparent self-reflection were hard to discern, but the 2009 expenses episode in the UK undoubtedly prompted UK parliamentarians to fundamentally re-think their own position more than was the case in Germany. A crisis the extent of which few had seen before has led parliamentarians to be more careful than ever when viewing moral and ethical issues – and this will have much more effect on political culture in the UK than, for example, the Committee on Standards in Public Life did in the late 1990s. It may well be a case of 'what doesn't kill you makes you stronger', as UK MPs now exist in a moral and ethical environment that is almost undoubtedly as clean as it has ever been. Yet, in terms of prosecutions – the fourth and final point – it is Germany that is paradoxically ahead of the UK. It is in Germany where high profile business leaders have been caught and imprisoned/fined. Again, this may change in the UK over time, but as things stand the rate of prosecutions is lower than anti-corruption activists would like it to be.

Given all this, the picture in Germany and the UK is a mixed one. Neither country has attempted anti-corruption revolutions, but over the last 15 years there have been changes – to laws and regulations, as well as in attitudes and behaviour – that make a difference. That this might just be as good as we can reasonably expect will disappoint many. But it is certainly worth something.

Conclusion

This book has tried to shed light on one deceptively simple question; under which conditions do specific types of anti-corruption strategy work? As was to be expected, there is clearly not a succinct set of answers to this question, but the analysis presented here has nonetheless offered us a number of pointers. This conclusion will highlight what these pointers are before suggesting ways forward from here.

The book began in Chapter 1 by analysing the rise and development of the global anti-corruption industry. It illustrated that concerted international attempts to fight corruption remain, perhaps surprisingly, a relatively new phenomenon. It also illustrated that whilst anti-corruption certainly 'arrived' in the 1990s, its path to centre stage was not without controversy. Although a consensus was quickly established across much of the international policy community as to what the key drivers of corrupt practices were, and subsequently what should be done to snuff them out, by the early 2000s a strong lobby was developing that felt not only that these anti-corruption methods and approaches were not working, but, even worse, they were in many ways detrimental to the cause and, for some, bordering on the self-serving. The anti-corruption movement has subsequently found itself forced to reassess much of what it treated, through the 1990s, as self-evident common sense, questioning its own assumptions, ideological underpinnings and, subsequently, methods and strategies. Chapter 1 illustrated that influential though many of the international organisations (and the policies that they espouse) remain, anti-corruption attempts in the second decade of the 21st century are now much more nuanced and flexible than they were just a few years previously.

Chapter 2 moved on to analyse how the need to understand governance regimes and local opportunity structures became so important before illustrating how this book uses work on hypothesised linkages between governance and corruption to shape the three empirical chapters. Whilst measuring governance is a process that is as fraught with difficulty as measuring corruption, there have been real advances in recent years and data such as those produced in the World Governance Indicators (WGI) can be useful starting points for conducting qualitative research on specific types of anti-corruption regime or policy, as well as on individual countries. The WGI indicators have come in for plenty of criticism, but they remain a useful tool for assisting us in making cross-country comparisons and for evaluating progress (or lack thereof) over time. Dan Kaufmann and his colleagues are well aware that they are 'too blunt a tool to be useful in formulating specific governance reforms in particular country contexts' and that country-specific, qualitative analysis is vital in pinpointing what anti-corruption strategies are likely to work and when.[1] It is to precisely this challenge – the need to do theoretically informed analysis of indicative cases – that this book takes up in Chapters 3, 4 and 5.

Chapter 3 looked at corruption and anti-corruption in two states with low quality governance structures. It illustrated that, to put it mildly, fighting corruption in countries where it is systemic and deeply engrained into political life is a challenge. And a challenge that very few politicians and/or political actors are likely – for a variety of reasons – to be able to meet. Chapter 3 illustrated this by looking at two cases, Bangladesh and Kenya, that, whilst in many ways very different, have faced broadly similar sets of governance dilemmas. Chapter 4 moved on to look at two states with moderately good governance infrastructures; South Korea and Poland. Corruption in these states remains a prominent feature of public discourse, but it has not prevented both states from making, at times, impressive economic progress. Chapter 5 moved the discussion on further by looking at two states with (generally) good governance infrastructures; Germany and the UK. In these states, as was the case across much of the western world until recently, elites have traditionally viewed their countries as being largely exempt from discourses on corruption, and that as it was perceived as being largely under control. Corruption was never taken to be non-existent or irrelevant, but it was, for much of the post-war period, seen as something that happened largely as bad applies enriched themselves but where systems of oversight, compliance and cultures of 'doing the right thing' would ultimately prevail. Chapter 5 illustrated that whilst there remain lingering doubts about commitment to genuine reform, much *has* changed in recent years – and that even though both countries still face significant corruption challenges.

What have these case studies told us about fighting corruption in these very different contexts? In the cases of countries where governance quality is low – and that unfortunately applies to most of the planet – the Kenyan and Bangladeshi experiences reveal a number of things. Firstly, there is always a political dimension to tackling corruption. Without 'buy in' from prominent stakeholders top-down attempts to cleanse public life are destined not just to fail but to fail badly. Anti-corruption is, by definition, political. The attempts of international organisations and well-meaning anti-corruption activists to talk about best practice and benchmarks are highly unlikely to bring with them genuine change. Change occurs when (often newly empowered) institutions successfully manage to walk the tightrope that links the ideals of those working there with the interests of the political actors that they are trying to influence. The partial success of Bangladesh's electoral commission is a good indicator of how this can work in practice. Persuading all parties to comply with registration requirements was certainly a considerable achievement, and there can be little doubt that they acceded to this demand because the commission sought dialogue and talked a language they could understand. Adopting a Right to Information Act in 2009, a Whistleblower Protection Act in 2011, and establishing both an Information Commission in 2009 and a Human Rights Commission (in 2007) have, despite the difficulties in actually implementing the provisions in them, also clearly been steps in the right direction. The key therefore may well be to fight corruption by essentially not talking about it. Anti-Corruption Agencies, new anti-corruption laws and so forth largely failed in Bangladesh – much as the literature would expect them to. It is the softer issues that have more chance of success, and in that context the experience of Bangladesh largely fits into what we might have expected.

The case of Kenya, meanwhile, is one of plentiful anti-corruption talk and disappointingly little anti-corruption substance. The introduction of a new constitution in 2010 may offer a ray of hope, and some of the changes, whilst not framed in anti-corruption language, may have a more sustainable impact on corruption in practice. Moves towards Freedom of Information, whilst still only tentative, also look much more promising than much of the anti-corruption legislation that was passed over the last decade. That Kenyan political elites superficially bought into much of the theoretical discourse on how to tackle corruption cannot disguise the fact that vested interests always short-circuited the system if their interests were threatened. Persuading them that change is not just in the best interests of the country but that it does not explicitly threaten them is – unpalatable as it may seem – an important part of the anti-corruption battle in Kenya that has not yet been won.

South Korea and Poland, meanwhile, do possess a fair degree of what one might call 'governance competence'. The quality of governance is mixed, and both South Korea and Poland perform well in some areas and less well in others. This has certainly not been an outright block on economic development and both states have subsequently created models that have enabled significant levels of corruption to go hand-in-hand with economic growth. Assessing progress in South Korea and Poland is subsequently difficult. Both the WGI and CPI data indicate improvements, but when margins of error are factored in (or assumed) then the extent of these improvements is not clear. Citizens in both countries certainly continue to view their politicians with suspicion and to be widely suspicious of politicians' (regular) claims that they are going to clean up public life.

Politicians in both countries have, in their own ways, looked to implement similar anti-corruption mechanisms – with at times quite different results. Both claimed to want to shake up civil service appointments, with the Polish PiS taking a particularly radical stance in this regard. The PiS argued explicitly that it wanted Poles to know who the public servants were that were serving them, and it moved to place those sympathetic to the PiS's cause in positions of influence. It was open about this and sold it as a way of increasing levels of both transparency and accountability. Whether this has enhanced attempts to tackle corrupt practices is a moot point, with the PiS's opponents claiming that the party simply (further) politicised the civil service for no discernible anti-corruption gain. There would, of course, be a way of passing judgement on all of this – create institutions with the mandate and resources to audit the performance and behaviour of civil servants. Given that this has not really happened it has been hard to pass definitive judgement, but the work of specialists in the area leaves plenty of room to believe that there is, at the very least, further reform necessary.

Where Poland arguably made more progress than South Korea, however, is in terms of its anti-corruption agency. Both states introduced a high profile ACA, and although the Polish CBA started off controversially and was widely criticised as being a tool of the then governing party, it did slowly develop in to an organisation that could make at least a partial impact. The story in South Korea is altogether different, and by the time the ACA there was merged with other bodies in 2008 it had long since ceased to be a genuine force for change. The Polish CBA was able to impose itself, it was able to ask awkward questions – that it did not do so to everyone's liking is not the point, it did at least begin to shake things up.

Where South Korea has done rather more impressively than Poland is in terms of empowering citizens to actively get involved with anti-corruption activity. Polish citizens condemn corruption, but they appear to be very reluctant to actively get involved in doing something about it. Through the 2000s Polish parties may well have discussed corruption a great deal, but civil society participation in combatting it never got much beyond the rhetorical level. In South Korea, meanwhile, a significant number of anti-corruption NGOs have engaged with policy-makers to try and change the political environment. They have pushed for the increased accountability of ministers and they have aggressively called for more transparency in business links with politics. They have clearly not been completely successful, but the murky world of 'chaebol' dominance is now at least a little less murky than it once was.

The cases of South Korea and Poland are in many ways frustrating. At times, political elites have appeared genuinely enthusiastic about anti-corruption reform. This enthusiasm has rarely lasted long or, indeed, led to demonstrable improvements in the anti-corruption framework. This is reflected in the patchy WGI scores that both states have registered. One thing that may well be worth bearing in mind is that anti-corruption rhetoric may well sound good in election campaigns, as was the case for the PiS in the mid-2000s, but it rarely leads to effective post-election anti-corruption policies. The PiS raised unrealistic expectations in Poland, rendering its substantives reforms always liable to underwhelm. Progress is often made when expectations are lower (or, arguably, more realistic) and governments can discuss, analyse and ultimately bring in their policies in less confrontational atmospheres.

Germany and the UK are, of course, in different positions again. Their strong institutional frameworks generally do good jobs of preventing corruption from taking place and when it does occur they possess, at least in theory, the tools to do something about it. That they nonetheless have specific anti-corruption challenges to deal with is not disputed, but the solutions tend to involve much more subtlety and nuance rather than radical change.

In terms of sharpening up the legal infrastructure, British attempts have been more radical than those undertaken in Germany. Germany has updated its legal infrastructure, but largely in piecemeal ways that build directly on pre-existing laws. The fact that Britain had not updated its legal anti-corruption framework for the best part of a century played a role in making the UK's recent legal innovations look more radical. In terms of teasing out more transparency in the area of financial accountability, Germany has been more proactive than the UK. Significant parts of German business, for so long praised for its efficiency and effectiveness both at home and abroad, were revealed to have serious corruption-related problems, and scandals involving some of the very biggest names have prompted changes (the true extent of which can be argued over) in both business culture and also the demands that regulators and prosecutors put on companies. The introduction of the UKBA in 2010 has propelled Britain to the very forefront of good practice in this area, although it will inevitably take time before the impact of this groundbreaking piece of legislation can be discerned. Be that as it may, the Act clearly focuses on financial practices in ways that many companies are suspicious of – and in and of itself this may be a good indication that the Act is putting financial transactions under the microscope that would otherwise never have seen the light of day.

Neither country has seen fit to bring in an anti-corruption agency, and neither looks likely to do so in the future – and that even though there may be a reasonable case in the UK for doing just that. However, this core part of the (theoretical) anti-corruption toolkit for states with good governance quality does not look like it is going to find much resonance over and beyond Germany and the UK; the institutions in states such as these generally work, and the radical changes that would come with magicing an ACA out of nowhere sit uneasily with the way these states are currently governed. It may be worth putting ideas of ACAs on the back burner for now as incremental change is almost always likely, in states that fit into the good quality governance category, to win out.

The almost never-ending stream of scandals in both Germany and the UK has led public servants to review their own moral and ethical behaviour. Given the changes that we have recently seen in the media landscape (i.e. the advent of 24/7 news via a plethora of new channels) and the rise of investigative journalism, this should come as no surprise. Being a frontline politician is now a job where you are never allowed a bad day, where one tweet can signal the end of your career and where you must always behave appropriately (even when you may well not be sure what exactly that means). Even the most capable of politicians will fall at one of these hurdles at some point. Yet, until the late 2000s the results of this apparent self-reflection were hard to discern. Politicians certainly became more professional, but in the UK at least it was not until the 2009 parliamentary expenses episode that British parliamentarians fundamentally reassessed their own behaviour. Germany had no such crisis, and has subsequently – despite talking a fair game – not made such obvious progress. The shear extent of the outrage that UK parliamentarians witnessed scared many of them in ways they will never have conceived possible before – and it is this sense of being so clearly on the wrong side of public opinion that prompted a reassessment. Long-standing democracies therefore need what Durkheim famously called 'cases of deviance' to bring them back on the straight and narrow – more or less precisely as the UK experienced in 2008 and 2009.[2] Analysis of the UK case therefore indicates that processes of soft, and where necessary hard, ethics management are likely to be very high up the agenda of countries in this particular governance bracket.

Given all this, the picture in Germany and the UK is a mixed one. Neither country has attempted anti-corruption revolutions, but over the last 15 years there have been changes – to laws and regulations, as well as in attitudes and behaviour – that make a difference. That this might just be as good as we can reasonably expect will disappoint many. But it is certainly worth something.

Where does this leave the bigger picture of in terms of the simple question asked at the beginning – under what conditions do which type of anti-corruption strategy work? There are, unsurprisingly, no concrete answers. But it clearly is the case that governance matters and once the governance context has been understood, then, and only then, will more specific anti-corruption policies have a chance. In states where governance quality is low, then politicians have to be persuaded to buy in – whether that means directly, indirectly or at times almost unknowingly – to the anti-corruption agenda. The suggestions made by the likes of Shah and Schacter in this area made intuitive sense and there is strong evidence that enhancing citizen participation, strengthening the institutions of representative government and bolstering the rule of law will make a real difference. The challenge is how to persuade those who have vested interests in the system that they will not systematically lose out. This might well be very distasteful for anti-corruption activists who know just how badly leaders have behaved in the past, but it nonetheless is a fundamental part of any successful anti-corruption strategy.

In states with more mixed levels of governance quality, the challenges are different but no less complex. The South Korean case illustrated how apparently substantive changes to both the legal framework and the relationships between business leaders and the political class can look excellent on paper but can in reality paper over the cracks whilst business carries on much as normal. That progress has been made is undeniable, but persuading stakeholders to genuinely embrace change has again proved difficult. The Polish case has clear similarities. It may well be worth remembering that it has often taken those with good quality governance regimes decades, and in some cases centuries, to get where they are now. Their progress has usually been neither linear not straightforward. Given that, it should not come as a surprise that countries with relatively young democratic lives in rapidly changing socio-economic situations are taking time to build up their governance infrastructure.

In terms of those countries that essentially have the fewest problems with corruption, two points are worth noting. Firstly, complacency is

rarely a sensible policy position, and given the high salience of corruption issues it is worth taking note of how even countries such as the
UK can be rocked by sets of allegations as apparently inconsequential
as who should pay for a moat to be cleaned or a duckhouse to be built.
Ethics and 'doing the right thing' matter more now than they have
ever done before, and governments are well advised to set up codes
of conduct and institutional safeguards to reduce the possibility of
such scandals blowing political life off course.

Secondly, anti-corruption frameworks cannot be allowed to stay
still. What worked at one point in time may (sometimes surprisingly
quickly) not work again at a later point. In Germany and the UK
neither set of political elites have shown themselves to be keen on
radical institutional change, and in many ways this is no bad thing.
States in this category tend to have frameworks that have prevailed
over time and, by and large, this is as they do the jobs required of
them. But they still have to move with the times. Constant auditing
of the effectiveness of the institutional framework is vital so that small
changes can be made as and when required and the shock of a large
scandal coming like a bolt out of the blue subsequently remains small.
This is not just good for the political class, it is good for the country
as a whole. Ensuring that codes of conduct, ethics frameworks, legal
positions and so on are fit for purpose needs to be an on-going, itera-
tive process. The alternative is knee-jerk reactions that can frequently
be no better than what existed before.

Finally, and more generally, the increased interest in quantifying
contested concepts has helped push the issue of corruption on to the
high table of politics. No one sees corruption as being irrelevant any
more, and the quantifiers have played their part in achieving this goal.
However, the serious progress will now be made by using these yard-
sticks to delve deeply into individual cases. The most enlightened of
the quantifiers know this (and embrace it), but there are too few com-
paritivists who rise to the challenge. The toolkits now exist, it is up to
the political scientists to get their hands dirty and see how they work
in practice. This book clearly has not, and cannot, offer all the answers
– but it has hopefully shown that plenty can be learnt by using detailed
case studies to make sense of not just how the world should or could
work, but how it actually does.

Notes

Introduction

1 P. M. Heywood and I. Krastev (2006), 'Political scandals and corruption', in P. M. Heywood, E. Jones, M. Rhodes and U. Sedelmeier (eds) *Developments in European Politics* (Basingstoke: Palgrave). See also E. Brown and J. Cloke (2004), 'Neoliberal reform, governance and corruption in the South: Assessing the international anti-corruption crusade', *Antipode*, 36 (2): 272–294.

2 See M. Philp (1997), 'Defining political corruption', *Political Studies*, 45 (3): 440.

3 See http://www.transparency.org/news_room/faq/corruption_faq, accessed on 30 November 2011; http://stats.oecd.org/glossary/detail.asp?ID=4773, accessed on 30 November 2011.

4 C. Schiller (2000), *Improving Governance and Fighting Corruption: An IMF Perspective* (Washington D.C.: IMF, Fiscal Affairs Department), p.1.

5 World Bank (undated), *Helping Countries Combat Corruption: The Role of the World Bank* (Washington D.C.: World Bank). Available on http://www1. worldbank.org/publicsector/anticorrupt/corruptn/cor02.htm, accessed on 1 December 2011.

6 M. Khan (1996), 'A typology of corrupt transactions in developing countries', *IDS Bulletin*, 27 (2): 12; A. J. Heidenheimer, M. Johnston and V. T. LeVine (eds) (1989), *Political Corruption* (New Brunswick: Transaction Publishers), p.6.

7 A. Shlefier and R. Vishny (1993), 'Corruption', *Quarterly Journal of Economics*, 108 (3): 599–617.

8 S. Rose-Ackerman (1999), *Corruption and Government: Causes, Consequences and Reform* (Cambridge: CUP), p.75; R. Klitgaard (1998), 'International cooperation against corruption', *SPAN*, Sept/October: 38–41.

9 D. Kaufmann (2005), 'Myths and realities of governance and corruption', in *The Global Competitiveness Report 2005–2006* (New York: World Economic Forum, OUP), p.82.

10 See for example E. Brown and J. Cloke (2004), p.283.

11 See for example E. Harrison (2007), 'Corruption', *Development in Practice*, 17 (4/5): 672–674.

12 See G. Blundo and J. P. Olivier de Sardin (2000), 'La corruption comme terrain. Pour une approche socio-anthropologique', in G. Blundo (ed.) *Monnaier les Povoirs. Espaces, Méchanismes et Représentations de la Corruption* (Paris: Presses universitaires de France, nouveux cahiers de 1'IUED), 9. For a particularly illuminating set of practical examples from India of how public office and private roles can become very blurred see A. Gupta

(1995), 'Blurred boundaries: The discourse of corruption, the culture of politics, and the imagined state', *American Ethnologist*, 22 (2): 375–402.

13 See the following for an enlightening discussion of this in more detail; M. Philp (1997), 436–462; M. Philp (2006), 'Modelling political corruption in transition', in U. von Alemann (ed.) *Dimensionen politischer Korruption. Beiträge zum Stand der internationalen Forschung* (Wiesbaden: VSVerlag für Sozialwissenschaften), pp.91–108. See also J. A. Gardiner (1993), 'Defining corruption', *Corruption and Reform*, 7: 111–124.

14 J. S. Nye (1967), 'Corruption and political development: A cost-benefit analysis', *American Political Science Review*, 61 (2): 416.

15 For an interesting discussion on discerning whether politicians themselves really do have the will to carry these campaigns through or whether their anti-corruption rhetoric is in fact just a convenient political tool see D. W. Brinkerhoff and N. P. Kulibaba (1999), *Identifying and Assessing Political Will for Anti-Corruption Efforts* (Washington D.C.: USAID Working Paper, Number 13).

16 A. Shah (2007), 'Tailoring the fight against corruption to country circumstances', in A. Shah (ed.) *Performance Accountability and Combating Corruption* (Washington D.C.: World Bank), pp.233–254.

17 See A. Kelso (2009), 'Parliament on its knees: MPs' expenses and the crisis of transparency at Westminster', *Political Quarterly*, 80 (3): 329–338.

18 D. Kaufmann, A. Kraay and M. Mastruzzi (2009), *Governance Matters VIII* (Washington D.C.: World Bank Development Research Group, Policy Research Paper 4978), p.5.

19 D. Kaufmann, A. Kraay and M. Mastruzzi (2009), p.5.

20 For a particularly good summary of recent empirical research, see D. Treisman (2007), 'What have we learned about the causes of corruption from ten years of cross-national empirical research?', *Annual Review of Political Science*, 10: 211–244. For a more general (and detailed) review see O-H. Fjeldstad and J. C. Andvig (2001), *Corruption: A Review of Contemporary Research* (Bergen: CMI Report R).

21 See J. Hopkin and A. Rodriguez-Pose (2007), '"Grabbing Hand" or "Helping Hand"? Corruption and the Economic Role of the State', *Governance*, 20 (2): 190–191.

22 V. Tanzi (2000a), 'Corruption, growth and public finances', *IMF Working Papers*, WP/00/182.

23 IMF (2002), *The IMF's Approach to Promoting Good Governance and Combating Corruption* (Washington D.C.: IMF); World Bank (2004), *World Bank Anti-Corruption Strategy* (Washington D.C.: World Bank).

24 See S. Rose-Ackerman (1999).

25 See also J. Hopkin and A. Rodriguez-Pose (2007), p.191.

26 J. Hopkin and A. Rodriguez-Pose (2007), p.191 and p.200.

27 See Transparency International's much vaunted Corruption Perceptions Index (CPI) for evidence of this. http://cpi.transparency.org/cpi2011/results/, accessed on 1 December 2011.

28 J. Stiglitz (2002), *Globalization and its Discontents* (London: Allen Lane), p.54.

29   A. Shah (2007), pp.233–254.
30   For more analysis on this see V. Collingwood (ed.)(undated), *Good Governance and the World Bank*, available on http://www.ucl.ac.uk/dpu-projects/drivers_urb_change/urb_economy/pdf_glob_SAP/BWP_Govern ance_World%20Bank.pdf (accessed on 1 December 2011).
31   D. Kaufmann, A. Kraay and M. Mastruzzi (2009), p.5.
32   See A. Shah and M. Schachter (2004), 'Combating corruption: Look before you leap', *Finance and Development*, 41(4): 40–43. For the data see D. Kaufmann, A. Kraay and M. Mastruzzi (2009). See http://info.world-bank.org/governance/wgi/index.asp for this most up to date set of governance indicators and analysis.
33   D. Kaufmann (2010), 'Governance matters 2010: Worldwide Governance Indicators highlight governance successes, reversals and failures', available at http://www.brookings.edu/opinions/2010/0924_wgi_kaufmann.aspx, viewed on 6 November 2011.
34   The others are voice & accountability, political stability & absence of violence, government effectiveness, regulatory quality and rule of law. See Chapter 3 for further analysis.
35   D. Kaufmann (2005), p.87. J. Huther and A. Shah (2000), *Anti-Corruption Policies and Programs: A Framework for Evaluation* (Washington D. C.: World Bank, Policy Research Working Paper, 2501), p.12.
36   J. Huther and A. Shah (2000), pp.9–10. See also A. Ades and R. Di Tella (1996), 'The causes and consequences of competition: A review of recent empirical contributions', *IDS Bulletin*, 27 (2): 6–11; R. K. Goel and M. A. Nelson (1998), 'Corruption and government size: A disaggregated analysis', *Public Choice*, XCVII: 107–120; A. Brunetti and B. Weder (1998), *A Free Press is Bad News for Corruption* (Basel: Wirtschaftswissenschaft-liches Zentrum der Universität Basel, Discussion Paper, Number 9809).
37   J. Huther and A. Shah (2000), p.10 and p.12.

Chapter 1   The Rise and Rise of the Global Anti-Corruption Movement

1   S. Sampson (2008), 'Corruption and anti-corruption in South-East Europe: Landscapes and sites', in L. de Sousa, P. Larmour and B. Hindess (eds) *Governments, NGOs and Anti-Corruption: The New Integrity Warriors* (London: Routledge), p.175. For the speech itself see IMF (1996), 'Summary Proceedings of the 51st Annual Meeting of the Board of Governors' (Washington D.C.: IMF), p.27. Available at http://www.imf.org/exter-nal/pubs/ft/SUMMARY/51/pdf/part01.pdf, accessed on 5 December 2011.
2   See for example S. Sampson (2007), *Can the World Bank Do the Right Thing? When Anti-Corruption Movements Become Anti-Corruption Budget Lines*, paper for American Anthropological Association annual meeting, Washington D.C., November 2007. Available at http://www.lunduni-versity.lu.se/o.o.i.s?id= 12683&postid=1146197, accessed on 6 December 2011.

3   M. Johnston (2006), 'From Thucydides to Mayor Daley: Bad politics, and a culture of corruption', *P.S. Political Science and Politics*, 39 (4): 809.
4   See for example N. Leff (1964), 'Economic development through bureaucratic corruption', *American Behavioral Scientist*, 8 (3): 8–14; D. H. Bayley (1966), 'The effects of corruption in a developing nation', *Western Political Quarterly*, 19 (4): 719–732.
5   P. Perry (1997), *Political Corruption and Political Geography* (Aldershot: Ashgate), p.38.
6   S. Huntington (1968), *Political Order in Changing Societies* (New Haven: Yale University Press), p.59. See also E. Brown and J. Cloke (2004), 'Neoliberal reform, governance and corruption in the south: Assessing the international anti-corruption crusade', *Antipode*, 36 (2): 280.
7   E. Harrison (2007), 'Corruption', *Development in Practice*, 17 (4/5): 675.
8   For analysis of some of these see M. J. Bull and J. Newell (eds) (2003), *Corruption in Contemporary Politics* (Basingstoke: Palgrave).
9   See C. Hotchkiss (1998), 'The sleeping dog stirs: New signs of life in efforts to end corruption in international business', *Journal of Public Policy and Marketing*, 17 (1), 108–115; K. A. Elliot (2002), 'Corruption as an international policy problem', in A. J. Heidenheimer and M. Johnston (eds) *Political Corruption: Concepts and Contexts* (New Brunswick: Transaction Publishers), pp.925–941; D. Schmidt (2007), 'Anti-corruption: What do we know? Research on preventing corruption in the post-communist world', *Political Studies Review*, 5 (2): 202–232.
10 R. Williams (2000), 'Introduction', in R. Williams and A. Doig (eds) *Controlling Corruption* (Cheltenham: Edward Elgar, volume 4), p.xiii.
11 S. Andersson and P. M. Heywood (2009), 'The politics of perception: Use and abuse of Transparency International's approach to measuring corruption', *Political Studies*, 57 (4): 746.
12 M. Johnston (2005a), 'Measuring the new corruption rankings: Implications for analysis and reform', in A. J. Heidenheimer and M. Johnston (eds) *Political Corruption: Concepts and Contexts* (London: Transaction Publishers), pp.865–884.
13 See http://www.transparency.org/about_us, accessed on 6 December 2011.
14 S. Sampson (2010), 'Diagnostics: Indicators and transparency in the anti-corruption industry', in S. Jansen, E. Schroeter and N. Stehr (eds) *Transparenz: multidisziplinaere Durchsichten durch Phoenomene und Theorien des Undurchsichtigen* (Wiesbaden: VS Verlag), p.102.
15 http://www.transparency.ie/resources/cpi-2011, accessed on 6 December 2011.
16 See for example Transparency International (2011), *Transparency International Corruption Perceptions Index (CPI) 2011. A Short Methodological Note.* Available at http://www.transparency.ie/sites/default/files/Short%20methodological%20note%20CPI%202011%2025%20nov%2011.pdf, accessed on 6 December 2011.
17 See http://cpi.transparency.org/cpi2011/results/, accessed on 6 December 2011.

18   S. Andersson and P. M. Heywood (2009), pp.752–753.

19   S. Sampson (2007), pp.6–7.

20   S. Knack (2007), 'Measuring corruption: A critique of indicators in Eastern Europe and Central Asia', *Journal of Public Policy*, 27 (3): 263–265; T. Thompson and A. Shah (2005), *Transparency International's Corruption Perceptions Index: Whose Perceptions are They Anyway?* (Washington D.C.: World Bank).

21   T. Thompson and A. Shah (2005), pp.8–9.

22   S. Knack (2007), p.265.

23   S. Knack (2007), p.267.

24   See for example J. G. Lambsdorff (2005a), 'The methodology of the 2005 corruption perceptions index', available on http://www.icgg.org/downloads/CPI_Methodology.pdf, accessed on 6 December 2011; J. G. Lambsdorff (2005b), 'Determining trends for perceived levels of corruption' (Passau: University of Passau, Discussion Paper V-38-05).

25   See http://www.transparency.org/policy_research/surveys_indices/bpi and http://www.transparency.org/policy_research/surveys_indices/gcb, both accessed on 6 December 2011.

26   Quoted in S. Andersson and P. M. Heywood (2009), p.755.

27   M. Johnston (2005a), p.875.

28   S. Andersson and P. M. Heywood (2009), p.747.

29   E. Brown and J. Cloke (2004), p.275.

30   S. Andersson and P. M. Heywood (2009), p.747.

31   http://www.transparency.org/policy_research/surveys_indices/gcb/2010, accessed on 6 December 2011.

32   http://www.transparency.org/policy_research/surveys_indices/bpi/bpi_2008, accessed on 6 December 2011.

33   See for example D. Kaufmann, A. Kraay and M. Mastruzzi (2007), *The Worldwide Governance Indicators Project: Answering the Critics* (Washington D.C.: World Bank), p.1.

34   See http://www.ebrd.com/pages/research/analysis/surveys/beeps.shtml and http://www.weforum.org/issues/partnering-against-corruption-initiative, accessed on 8 December 2011.

35   See A. Lopez-Claros, M. E. Porter. and K. Schwab (2005), *Global Competitiveness Report, 2005–2006: Policies Underpinning Rising Prosperity* (Basingstoke: Palgrave Macmillan); IMD (2005), *World Competitiveness Yearbook, 2005* (Lausanne: IMD), available at http://www01.imd.ch/wcc/ranking/, accessed on 7 December 2011.

36   See http://www.worldvaluessurvey.org/ and http://rechten.uvt.nl/icvs/pdffiles/ICVS2004_05.pdf, both accessed on 7 December 2011. See also J. Svensson (2005), 'Eight questions about corruption', *Journal of Economic Perspectives*, 19 (3), 19–42.

37   See http://www.odi.org.uk/work/projects/00-07-world-governance-assessment/, http://www.uneca.org/itca/governance/Governance.htm and http://www.prsgroup.com/ICRG.aspx, all accessed on 7 December 2011. For a good overview of all these surveys see S. Knack (2007), pp.257–259.

38   S. Sampson (2010), p.103.

39 See for example B. Michael (2007), *The Rise and Fall of the Anti-Corruption Industry: Toward Second Generation Anti-Corruption Reforms in Central and Eastern Europe* (Paris: France); E. Brown and J. Cloke (2004), p.274; S. Sampson (2008), p.170.

40 H. Moroff and D. Schmidt-Pfister (2010), 'Anti-corruption movements, mechanisms and machines – an introduction', *Global Crime*, 11 (2): 90.

41 B. Michael and D. Bowser (2009), *The Evolution of the Anti-Corruption Industry in the Third Wave of Anti-Corruption Work* (New York: Columbia University), p.1; B. Michael (2004), 'The rapid rise of the anti-corruption Industry', *Local Governance Brief* (Budapest: Open Society Institute).

42 B. Michael and D. Bowser (2009), p.3.

43 B. Michael and D. Bowser (2009), p.4.

44 B. Michael and D. Bowser (2009), pp.5–6.

45 H. Moroff and D. Schmidt-Pfister (2010), p.92.

46 S. Sampson (2008), p.171. See also A. Mungiu-Pippidi (2006), 'Corruption: Diagnosis and treatment', *Journal of Democracy*, 17 (3): 86–99.

47 D. Kaufmann (2009), 'Aid effectiveness and governance: The good, the bad and the ugly', *Development Outreach* (Washington D.C.: World Bank Institute, February), p.27.

48 J. Hopkin (2002), 'States, markets and corruption: A review of some recent literature', *Review of International Political Economy*, 9 (3): 574–576.

49 J. Hopkin, (2002), p.577. See also J. Buchanan, R. Tollison and G. Tullock (eds) (1980) *Toward a Theory of the Rent-Seeking Society* (College Station: Texas A & M Press).

50 A. Downs (1957), *An Economic Theory of Democracy* (New York: Harper and Row).

51 N. Zhong (2010), *The Causes, Consequences and Cures of Corruption: A Review of Issues* (Hong Kong: The Chinese University of Hong Kong), p.1. Available at http://www.usc.cuhk.edu.hk/PaperCollection/webmanager/wkfiles/7489_1_paper.pdf, accessed on 7 December 2011.

52 A. Alesina and G-M. Angeletos (2005), 'Corruption, inequality and fairness', *Journal of Monetary Economics*, 52 (7): 1241.

53 J. Hopkin (2002), p.580.

54 N. Zhong (2010), p.2. Available at http://www.usc.cuhk.edu.hk/PaperCollection/webmanager/wkfiles/7489_1_paper.pdf, accessed on 7 December 2011.

55 See for example S. Rose-Ackerman (1978), *Corruption: A Study in Political Economy* (New York: Academic Press); C. Rowley, R. Tollison and G. Tullock (eds) (1989), *The Political Economy of Rent-Seeking* (Boston: Kluwer); S. Rose-Ackerman (1999), *Corruption and Government: Causes, Consequences and Reform* (Cambridge: Cambridge University Press); V. Tanzi (2000b), *Policies, Institutions and the Dark Side of Economics* (Cheltenham: Edward Elgar).

56 Quoted in N. Zhong (2010), p.2.

57 V. Tanzi (2000b), p.19.

58 V. Tanzi (2000b), p.133.

59 S. Rose-Ackerman (1999), pp.43–44.

60   J. Hopkin (2002), p.584.

61   J. Hopkin (2002), p.577.

62   J. Saxton (1999), *Can IMF Lending Promote Corruption?* (Washington D.C.: US Congress, Joint Economic Committee), p.1.

63   See United Nations (1996), *General Assembly Declaration Against Corruption and Bribery in International Commercial Transactions*, Document A/RES/51/191. Available at http://www.un.org/documents/ga/res/51/a51r191.htm, accessed on 8 December 2011. See also M. Bukovansky (2006), 'The hollowness of anti-corruption discourse', *Review of International Political Economy*, 13 (2): 186–187.

64   M. Pieth (1997), 'Contributions of industrialised countries in the prevention of corruption: The example of the OECD', speech given at the 8th International Anti-Corruption Conference, 7–11 September, available at http://iacconference.org/documents/8th_iacc_workshop_Contribution_of_Industrialised_Countries_in_the_Prevention_of_Corruption_The_Example_of_the_OECD.pdf, accessed on 8 December 2011. See also Organization for Economic Co-operation and Development (1997), *OECD Convention on Combating Bribery of Foreign Public Officials in International Business Transactions* (Paris: OECD).

65   M. Bukovansky (2006), p.191.

66   See for example International Monetary Fund (1997b), *IMF Adopts Guidelines Regarding Governance Issues* (Washington D.C.: IMF News Brief, No. 97/15), available at http://www.imf.org/external/np/sec/nb/1997/NB9715.HTM, accessed on 8 December 2011; P. Mauro (1995), 'Corruption and growth', *Quarterly Journal of Economics*, 110(3): 681–712; P. Mauro (1997) *Why Worry About Corruption?* (Washington D.C.: IMF, Economic Issues Series, Number 6); A. Shleifer and R. W. Vishny (1993), 'Corruption', *Quarterly Journal of Economics*, 108 (3): 599–617; V. Tanzi (1994), *Corruption, Government Activities and Markets* (Washington D.C.: IMF, Working Paper 94/99); V. Tanzi and H. Davoodi (1998), *Roads to Nowhere: How Corruption in Public Investment Hurts Growth* (Washington D. C.: IMF, Economic Issues Series, number 12); F. Vogl (1998), 'The supply side of global bribery', *Finance and Development*, 35 (2): 55–64.

67   Interim Committee Declaration (1996a), *Partnership for Sustainable Global Growth* (Washington D.C.: IMF); See also International Monetary Fund (1997a) *The Role of the IMF in Governance Issues – Guidance Note* (Washington D.C.: IMF), available at http://www.imf.org/external/np/sec/nb/1997/NB9715.HTM, accessed on 8 December 2011.

68   M. Bukovansky (2006), p.190. See also International Monetary Fund (2003), *IMF and Good Governance: A Factsheet* (Washington D.C.: IMF), available at http://www.imf.org/external/np/exr/facts/gov.htm, accessed on 8 December 2011.

69   See C. Schiller (2000), *Improving Governance and Fighting Corruption: An IMF Perspective* (Washington D.C.: IMF) for a good summary of what the IMF believes corruption's negative effects to be. Available on http://www.oas.org/juridico/english/imf2000.htm, accessed on 8 December 2011.

70   See C. Schiller (2000).

71   V. Tanzi (1994); V. Tanzi (1998), *Corruption Around the World: Causes, Consequences, Scope and Cures* (Washington D.C.: IMF, Working Paper 98/63), pp.3 and 10–16.

72   A significant body of research rejected this even before the Bank started talking explicitly about corruption. See for example D. Gillies (1996), 'Human rights, democracy and good governance: Stretching the World Bank's policy frontiers', in J. Griesgraber and B. Gunter (eds) *The World Bank: Lending on a Global Scale* (London: Pluto Press), pp.104–141; M. Miller-Adams (1999), *The World Bank: New Agendas in a Changing World* (London: Routledge).

73   H. Marquette (2004), 'The creeping politicisation of the World Bank: The case of corruption', *Political Studies*, 52(3): 413; World Bank (1997), *Helping Countries Combat Corruption: The Role of the World Bank* (Washington D.C.: World Bank), p.2.

74   See M. Szeftel (1998), 'Misunderstanding African politics: Corruption and the governance agenda', *Review of African Political Economy*, 76: 221–240; E. Brown and J. Cloke (2004), p.286.

75   S. Riley (1998), 'The political economy of anti-corruption strategies in Africa', in M. Robinson (ed.) *Corruption and Development* (London: Frank Cass), p.138.

76   E. Brown and J. Cloke (2004), p.289.

77   H. Marquette (2004), p.413. See also H. Marquette (2003), *Corruption, Development and Politics: The Role of the World Bank* (Basingstoke: Palgrave).

78   A. Shah (2007), 'Tailoring the fight against corruption to country circumstances', in A. Shah (ed.) *Performance Accountability and Combating Corruption* (Washington D.C.: World Bank), p.234.

Chapter 2   Governance Regimes and the Fight against Corruption

1   For more on this in the specific context of development see B. C. Smith (2007), *Good Governance and Development* (Basingstoke: Palgrave).

2   C. Hewitt de Alcantara (1998), 'Uses and abuses of the concept of governance', *International Social Science Journal*, Number 155, p.106.

3   M. A. Thomas (2010), 'What do the Worldwide Governance Indicators measure?', *European Journal of Development of Research*, 22 (1): 31.

4   C. Hewitt de Alcantara (1998), p.105.

5   P. Norris (2010), 'Measuring governance', in M. Bevir (ed.) *Sage Handbook of Governance* (London: Sage), p.424.

6   C. Arndt and C. Oman (2006), *Uses and Abuses of Governance Indicators* (Paris: OECD Development Centre Study), p.11.

7   World Bank (1991), *Managing Development – The Governance Dimension* (Washington D.C.: World Bank), p.1; UNDP (1997), *Governance for Sustainable Human Development* (New York: UNDP). Also available at

http://mirror.undp.org/magnet/policy/chapter1.htm#b, accessed on 13 December 2011.

8   World Bank (1992), *Governance and Development* (Washington, D.C.: World Bank), p.1; World Bank (1994), *Governance: The World Bank's Experience* (Washington, D.C.: World Bank), p.vii.

9   World Bank (2007), *Strengthening World Bank Group Engagement on Governance and Anticorruption* (Washington D.C.: World Bank, Joint Ministerial Committee of the Boards of Governors of the Bank and the Fund on the Transfer of Real Resources to Developing Countries), p.1.

10 See OECD (2007), *Glossary of Statistical Terms*, available at http://stats.oecd.org/glossary/detail.asp?ID=7236, accessed on 13 December 2011; UNESCAP (2011), *What is Good Governance?* (New York: United Nations), p.1.

11 IMF (2005), *The IMF's Approach to Promoting Good Governance and Combating Corruption – A Guide* (New York: IMF). See also http://www.imf.org/external/ np/gov/guide/eng/index.htm, accessed on 11 December 2011.

12 C. Gibson (undated), *Governance, Political Science and the Environment*, available at http://www2.bren.ucsb.edu/~gsd/Gibson_Governance_and_political_science.pdf, p.1.

13 D. Kaufman and A. Kraay (2008), 'Governance indicators: Where are we, where should we be going?', *The World Bank Research Observer*, 23 (1): 4.

14 See D. Kaufmann, A. Kraay and P. Zoido-Lobatón (1999), *Aggregating Governance Indicators* (Washington D.C.: World Bank, Policy Research Working Paper 2195), p.1. See also D. Kaufmann, A. Kraay and M. Mastruzzi (2009), *Governance Matters VIII* (Washington D.C.: World Bank Development Research Group, Policy Research Paper 4978), p.4.

15 M. Andrews (2010), 'Good government means different things in different countries', *Governance*, 23 (1): 7.

16 S. Andersson and P. M. Heywood (2009), 'The politics of perception: Use and abuse of Transparency International's approach to measuring corruption', *Political Studies*, 57 (4): 751.

17 S. Andersson and P. M. Heywood (2009), p. 751. For a good discussion of this see also C. Hewitt de Alcantara (1998), pp.105–113.

18 M. Bukovansky (2006), 'The hollowness of anti-corruption discourse', *Review of International Political Economy*, 13 (2): 183.

19 B. Rothstein (2011), 'Anti-corruption: The indirect "big bang" approach', *Review of International Political Economy*, 18 (2): 235.

20 M. Philp (2006), 'Modelling political corruption in transition', in U. von Alemann (ed.) *Dimensionen politischer Korruption. Beiträge zum Stand der internationalen Forschung* (Wiesbaden: VS Verlag), p.97.

21 B. Rothstein (2011), p.235. See also D. Falaschetti and G. Miller (2001), 'Constraining the Leviathan: Moral hazard and credible commitment in constitutional design', *Journal of Theoretical Politics*, 13 (4): 389–411; S. Fritzen (2003), *The 'Misery' of Implementation: Governance, Institutions and Anti-Corruption in Vietnam*, paper for conference on 'Governance,

institutions and anti-corruption in Asia', New Zealand Asia Institute, University of Auckland, April 2003. Available at http://goodgovernance. bappenas.go.id/publikasi_CD/cd_penerapan/ref_cd_penerapan/download/unfolder/Governance.anti-corruption.pdf, accessed on 13 December 2011.

22 H. Roberts (2003), *Political Corruption in and Beyond the Nation State* (London: Routledge), p.63.

23 For information on Freedom House's work in this area see http://www.freedomhouse.org; for a good summary of the use of indicators in measuring different aspects of governance see P. Norris (2010), pp.411–457.

24 P. Norris (2010), p.413; C. Arndt and C. Oman (2006), p.11.

25 See for example UNDP (2007), *Governance Indicators: A Users' Guide* (Oslo: UNDP, 2nd edition).

26 See in particular M. A. Thomas (2010), pp.36–37; S. Knack (2007), 'Measuring corruption: A critique of indicators in Eastern Europe and Central Asia', *Journal of Public Policy*, 27 (3): 276–282.

27 C. Arndt and C. Oman (2006).

28 See C. Arndt and C. Oman (2006); S. Knack (2007), pp.264–265; see also M. A. Thomas (2010), pp.42–51.

29 See for example E. Glaeser, R. LaPorta, F. Lopez-de-Silanes and A. Shleifer (2004), 'Do institutions cause growth?, *Journal of Economic Growth*, 9 (3): 271–303; S. Knack (2007), p.282. For a rebuttal of this point see D. Kaufmann, A. Kraay and M. Mastruzzi (2007), *The Worldwide Governance Indicators Project: Answering the Critics* (Washington D.C.: World Bank), p.15.

30 Melissa Thomas provides a particularly good example of this, see M. A. Thomas (2010), pp.31–54.

31 P. Norris (2010), p.424.

32 Daniel Kaufmann and colleagues have produced a significant number of documents on WGI approaches, methods and of course findings. Some of the most significant include D. Kaufmann, A. Kraay and P. Zoido-Lobatón (1999); D. Kaufmann, A. Kraay and M. Mastruzzi (2007); D. Kaufman and A. Kraay (2008), pp.1–30; D. Kaufmann, A. Kraay and M. Mastruzzi (2009).

33 These indicators are explained in virtually identical ways in all of reports on the WGI. See for example D. Kaufmann, A. Kraay and M. Mastruzzi (2009), p.6.

34 D. Kaufmann, A. Kraay and M. Mastruzzi (2009), p.4.

35 See http://www.govindicators.org, accessed on 11 December 2011.

36 D. Kaufmann, A. Kraay and M. Mastruzzi (2009), p.2.

37 They claim that the only other governance related indices that report margins of error are the TI CPI and the Global Integrity Index. See D. Kaufmann, A. Kraay and M. Mastruzzi (2009), p.3.

38 D. Kaufmann, A. Kraay and M. Mastruzzi (2009), p.2.

39 See, for example, C. Arndt and C. Oman (2006); S. Knack (2007), pp.255–291; M. A. Thomas (2010), pp.31–54.

40 For a robust rebuttal of these criticisms see D. Kaufmann, A. Kraay and M. Mastruzzi (2007).

41 For a particularly interesting analysis of this see C. Arndt and C. Oman (2006), pp.65–67.

42 D. Kaufmann, A. Kraay and M. Mastruzzi (2007), p.30.

43 S. Knack (2007), pp.264–265. See also C. Arndt and C. Oman (2006), pp.66–67.

44 For a detailed explanation of this see D. Kaufmann, A. Kraay and M. Mastruzzi (2007), pp.3–4.

45 C. Arndt and C. Oman (2006), p.67.

46 D. Kaufmann, A. Kraay and M. Mastruzzi (2007), p.4.

47 S. Knack (2007), p.258; C. Arndt and C. Oman (2006), p.69.

48 Kaufmann et al. actually outline what types of business were included in the surveys they use, illustrating that small businesses (as opposed to global multi-nationals) tend to be very well represented. D. Kaufmann, A. Kraay and M. Mastruzzi (2007), pp.12–13.

49 S. Knack (2007), p.263.

50 C. Arndt and C. Oman (2006), p.72.

51 M. A. Thomas (2010), p.51.

52 D. Kaufmann, A. Kraay and M. Mastruzzi (2007), p.27.

53 D. Kaufmann (2010), *Governance Matters 2010: World Governance Indicators Highlight Governance Successes, Reversals and Failures*, 24 September, available on http://www.brookings.edu/opinions/2010/0924_wgi_kaufmann. aspx, accessed on 13 December 2011.

54 D. Kaufmann (2010).

55 A. Shah (2007), 'Tailoring the fight against corruption to country circumstances', in A. Shah (ed.) *Performance Accountability and Combating Corruption* (Washington D.C.: World Bank), p.235; E. Harrison (2007), 'Corruption', *Development in Practice*, 17 (4/5): 672.

56 J. Huther and A. Shah (2000), *Anti-Corruption Policies and Programmes: A Framework for Evaluation* (Washington D.C.: World Bank, Policy Research Working Paper 2501), p.9. See also A. Shah and M. Schacter (2004), 'Combating corruption: Look before you leap', *Finance and Development*, 41 (4): 42.

57 A. Shah and M. Schacter (2004), p.42.

58 D. Smilov (2010), 'Anticorruption agencies: Expressive, constructivist and strategic uses', *Crime, Law and Social Change*, 53 (1): 67–77.

59 A. Shah and M. Schacter (2004), p.42.

60 Adapted from J. Huther and A. Shah (2000), p.12.

61 A. Shah and M. Schacter (2004), p.41.

62 A. Doig (2009), 'Markets, management, managed work and measurement: Setting the context for effective anti-corruption commissions', in L. de Sousa, P. Larmour and B. Hindess (eds) *Governments, NGOs and Anti-Corruption: The New Integrity Warriors* (London: Routledge/ECPR Studies in European Political Science); T. Gurgur and A. Shah (1999), 'The causes of corruption' (Washington D.C.: World Bank); D. Treisman (2007), 'What have we learned about the causes of corruption from ten

years of cross-national empirical research?', *Annual Review of Political Science*, 10: 211–244.

63   R. Stapenhurst (2000), *The Media's Role in Curbing Corruption* (Washington D.C.: World Bank); A. Brunetti and B. Weder (2003), 'A free press is bad news for corruption', *Journal of Public Economics*, 87: 1801–1824; T. Gurgur and A. Shah (2002), 'Localization and corruption: Panacea or Pandora's Box?', in E. Ahmed and V. Tanzi (eds) *Managing Fiscal Decentralization* (London: Routledge), pp.46–67; K. A. Elliott (1997), 'Corruption as an international policy problem: Overview and recommendations', in K. A. Elliott (ed.) *Corruption and the Global Economy* (Washington D.C.: Institute for International Economics).

64   This is particularly true in the area of anti-corruption mechanisms which have now received considerable coverage. See for example L. De Sousa (2010), 'Anti-corruption agencies: Between empowerment and irrelevance', *Crime, Law and Social Change*, 53: 5–22; A. Doig (1995), 'Good government and sustainable anti-corruption strategies: A role for independent anti-corruption agencies?', *Public Administration and Development*, 15 (2): 151–165; A. Doig, D. Watt and R. Williams (2007), 'Why developing country anticorruption agencies fail to develop', *Public Administration and Development*, 27 (3): 251–259; M. Johnston (1999), 'A brief history of anticorruption agencies', in A. Schedler, L. Diamond and M. F. Plattner (eds) *The Self-Restraining State: Power and Accountability in New Democracies* (Boulder, CO: Lynne Rienner), pp.217–226; D. Smilov (2010), pp.67–77.

65   J. Huther and A. Shah (2000), pp.9–10. See also A. Ades and R. Di Tella (1996), 'The causes and consequences of competition: A review of recent empirical contributions', *IDS Bulletin*, 27 (2): 6–11; R. K. Goel and M. A. Nelson (1998), 'Corruption and government size: A disaggregated analysis', *Public Choice*, XCVII: 107–120; A. Brunetti and B. Weder (1998), *A Free Press is Bad News for Corruption* (Basel: Wirtschaftswissenschaftliches Zentrum der Universität Basel, Discussion Paper, Number 9809).

66   J. Huther and A. Shah (2000), pp.10–12.

Chapter 3   Bangladesh and Kenya: Tough Talk, Small Steps, Ineffectual Outcomes

1   J. Roberts and S. Fagernäs (2004), *Why is Bangladesh Outperforming Kenya? A Comparative Study of Growth and Its Causes Since the 1960s* (London: Overseas Development Institute, ESAU Working Paper 5), p.1.

2   Iftekharuzzaman and T. Mahmud (2008), 'Bangladesh', in Transparency International, *Global Corruption Report 2008* (Cambridge: CUP), p.184; Polity IV (2011), *Polity IV Country Report 2010: Kenya*, available at http://systemicpeace.org/polity/Kenya2010.pdf, viewed on 3 January 2012, p.2.

3   For more information on the data sources used here, see http://info.world-bank.org/governance/wgi/pdf/cc.pdf, viewed on 28 December 2011.

4   J. S. T. Quah (1999), 'Comparing anti-corruption measures in Asian countries: Lessons to be learnt', *Asian Review of Public Administration*, XI (2), July–December: 76.

5   C. Knox (2009), 'Dealing with sectoral corruption in Bangladesh: Developing citizen involvement', *Public Administration and Development*, 29: 120.

6   H. Zafarullah and R. Rahman (2008), 'The impaired state: Assessing state capacity and governance in Bangladesh', *International Journal of Public Sector Management*, 21 (7): 742.

7   A. Zakiuddin (undated), *Corruption in Bangladesh: An Analytical and Sociological Study*, available on http://www.ti-bangladesh.org/docs/research/CorBang1.htm, viewed on 29 December 2011, here p.3.

8   M. M. Khan (1998), *Administrative Reforms in Bangladesh* (New Delhi: South Asian Publications), p.35.

9   Iftekharuzzaman (2005), 'Corruption and human insecurity in Bangladesh', paper presented at Transparency International Bangladesh Anti-Corruption Day held in Dhaka, 9 December, p.23. Available at http://www.ti-bangladesh.org/research/Corruption&HumanSecurity091205.pdf, viewed on 29 December 2011.

10 C. Knox (2009), p.120.

11 M. Momen (2009), 'Bangladesh in 2008: Déjà vu again or a return to democracy?', *Asian Survey*, 49 (1): 72.

12 For more on caretaker governments in Bangladesh see N. Ahmed (2010), 'Party politics under a non-party caretaker government in Bangladesh: The Fakhruddin interregnum', *Commonwealth and Comparative Politics*, 48 (1): 23–27.

13 Iftekharuzzaman and T. Mahmud (2008), p.183.

14 N. Ahmed (2010), p.24 and p.26.

15 Iftekharuzzaman and T. Mahmud (2008), p.184.

16 J. Johnson (2007), 'Bangladesh generals plan anti-corruption drive', *Financial Times*, 16 January.

17 M. Momen (2009), p.13.

18 Iftekharuzzaman and T. Mahmud (2008), p.184.

19 M. H. Khan (2010), 'Corruption and governance in South Asia', in *Europa South Asia Yearbook 2009* (London: Europa, unpublished), p.7. Available at http://eprints.soas.ac.uk/11683/1/Corruption_and_Governance_in_South_Asia_2009.pdf, viewed on 28 December 2011.

20 Iftekharuzzaman and T. Mahmud (2008), p.182.

21 For more on this, see Iftekharuzzaman and T. Mahmud (2008), pp.182–183.

22 N. Ahmed (2010), p.32.

23 Transparency International Bangladesh (2010), *Annual Report 2009* (Dhaka: Transparency International), p.13.

24 See for example the 18 recommendations that TIB made in March 2011; Transparency International Bangladesh (2011b), *Making the Anti-Corruption Commission Effective* (Dhaka: TIB, Policy Brief).

25   See 'Muhammad Yunus and Bangladesh: Forced out', *The Economist*, 5 April 2011; 'Bangladesh looks back: Misusing the past', *The Economist*, 1 August 2011.

26   Sheikh Hasina, quoted in 'Ensure free flow of info', *The Daily Star*, 8 August 2009, available on http://www.thedailystar.net/newDesign/ news-details.php?nid=100432, viewed on 6 January 2012; see also 'Bill passed to protect whistleblowers', *The Daily Star*, 7 June 2011, available on http://www.thedailystar.net/newDesign/news-details.php?nid=188979, viewed on 6 January 2012.

27   Transparency International Bangladesh (2011b), p.30.

28   P. Landell-Mills (1999), 'Mobilizing civil society to fight corruption in Bangladesh', *World Bank PremNotes*, October, 30, p.1.

29   For a fuller analysis of TIB's work see TIB's annual reports, all of which are available on its website; http://www.ti-bangladesh.org/, viewed on 29 December 2011.

30   C. Knox (2009), p.126.

31   Transparency International Bangladesh (2011b), p.4.

32   Transparency International Bangladesh (2010), p.7.

33   Transparency International Bangladesh (2010), p.34.

34   Transparency International Bangladesh (2011b), p.8.

35   Transparency International Bangladesh (2011b), p.10.

36   Transparency International Bangladesh (2011b), p.23.

37   Iftekharuzzaman and M. S. Hussein (2010), *Integrity Pledge: Participatory Governance through Social Accountability* (Dhaka: Transparency International), p.2; Transparency International Bangladesh (2010), p.10; Transparency International Bangladesh (2011b), p.10.

38   C. Knox (2009), p.128.

39   Transparency International Bangladesh (2011b), p.7 and p.12.

40   Transparency International Bangladesh (2010), pp.32–33.

41   A. Palmer (2011), 'A new future for Kenya: Reforming a culture of corruption', *Harvard International Review*, Winter, p.32.

42   See M. Bratton and N. van der Walle (1994), 'Neopatrimonial regimes and political transitions in Africa', *World Politics*, 46 (4): 453–489.

43   L. A. Cherotich (undated), *Corruption and Democracy in Kenya* (Amsterdam: Netherlands Institute for Multiparty Democracy), p.1. Available at http:// www.nimd.org/documents/C/corruption_and_democracy_in_kenya.pdf, viewed on 3 January 2012.

44   A. Palmer (2011), p.32.

45   Transparency International Kenya (2002), *After KACA What Next? Fighting Corruption in Kenya* (Nairobi: Transparency International-Kenya), p.81; L. V. O. Ogwang (2007), *Rethinking Kenya's Anti-Corruption Strategies: Lessons from Botswana* (Pretoria: University of Pretoria), p.18 and p.33.

46   African Peer Review Mechanism (2006), *Country Review Report of the Republic of Kenya* (Midrand, South Africa: African Peer Review Mechanism). Available at http://www.polity.org.za/article/aprm-country-review-report-of-the-republic-of-kenya-december-2006-20, downloaded on 3 January 2011), p.97.

47   J. T. Gathii (1999), 'Corruption and donor reforms: Expanding the promises and possibilities of the rule of law as an anti-corruption strategy in Kenya', *Connecticut Journal of International Law*, 14: 412.

48   M. Kibathi (2011), *Immediate Reforms Needed to Change the Image of Kenya Police* (Nairobi: TI Kenya). Available at http://tikenya.org/index.php? option=com_docman&task=doc_download&gid=92& Itemid=146, viewed on 4 January 2012.

49   In June 1997 the IMF refused to transfer funds intended to be part of the 'Enhanced Structural Adjustment Facility' citing both poor governance and corruption as the major cause. See J. T. Gathii (1999), p.407. See also J. Githongo (2005), 'Report on my findings of graft in the Government of Kenya', p. 16, available on http://www.africafocus.org/ docs06/git0602.php, viewed on 3 January 2011.

50   L. A. Cherotich (undated), p.1.

51   For more on the Anglo-Leasing scandal as well as corruption in Kenya more generally, see M. Wrong (2009), *Our Turn to Eat: The Story of a Kenyan Whistleblower* (New York: Harper) and G. Otieno (2005), 'The NARC's anti-corruption drive in Kenya: Somewhere over the rainbow?' *African Security Review*, 14 (2): 69–79. For more on the Goldenberg Affair see P. Warutere (undated), *Anatomy of a Scandal: Money, Power and the Winded Path of Goldenberg's Deals*, available at http://www.ipocafrica. org/index.php?option=com_content&view=article&id=69&Itemid=68, viewed on 3 January 2012.

52   L. Lawson (2009), 'The politics of anti-corruption reform in Africa', *Journal of Modern African Studies*, 47 (1): 79.

53   L. V. O. Ogwang (2007), *Rethinking Kenya's Anti-Corruption Strategies: Lessons from Botswana* (Pretoria: University of Pretoria), p.2.

54   C. K. Haarhuis (2005), *Promoting Anti-Corruption Reforms* (Utrecht: University of Utrecht, PhD thesis), p.67; Kenya Anti-Corruption Authority (2000), *National Anticorruption Plan 2000* (Nairobi: KACA).

55   J. P. Mutonyi (2002), 'Fighting corruption: Is Kenya on the right track?, *Police Practice & Research, An International Journal*, 3 (1): 30.

56   C. K. Haarhuis (2005), p.108.

57   Transparency International Kenya (2002), p.85.

58   C. Mullei and A. Mullei (2000), 'Corruption in the court system', in A. Mullei (ed.) *The Link Between Corruption and Poverty: Lessons from Kenya Case Studies* (Nairobi: African Centre for Economic Growth), p.117.

59   See for example C. K. Haarhuis (2005), p.71.

60   For more on the details of these policies/institutions, see L. V. O. Ogwang (2007), *Rethinking Kenya's Anti-Corruption Strategies: Lessons from Botswana* (Pretoria: University of Pretoria), pp.2–4, pp.22–23.

61   L. Lawson (2009), p.94; 'Key highlights from the EACC annual report 2010/2011' (2011), available on http://www.kacc.go.ke/whatsnew.asp? id=353, viewed on 4 January 2012.

62   L. Lawson (2009), p.79. For an excellent analysis both of this case and of corruption in Kenya see also M. Wrong (2009).

63   Quoted in '$47m of donor money stolen in Kenya', *The Irish Times*, 16 June 2011.

64   See A. Palmer (2011), p.33.

65   See 'Kenyan anger over corruption job', BBC News Online, available at http://news.bbc.co.uk/2/hi/africa/8231252.stm, viewed on 4 January 2012.

66   See 'Kenyan corruption chief resigns', BBC News Online, available at http://news.bbc.co.uk/2/hi/8283103.stm, viewed on 4 January 2012.

67   See A. Palmer (2011), p.34.

68   Quoted in '$47m of donor money stolen in Kenya', *The Irish Times*, 16 June 2011.

69   See 'Key highlights from the EACC annual report 2010/2011' (2011), available on http://www.kacc.go.ke/whatsnew.asp?id=353, viewed on 4 January 2012.

70   For a commentary on these see 'A chance to improve how Kenya is run', *The Economist*, 29 June 2010.

71   There is considerable dispute in the literature on tackling corruption as to whether devolving power is a good or bad thing. It may bring policy-making closer to the people and cut many of the most corrupt state-wide level politicians out of the process. This could lead to lower levels or corruption and more responsive government. However, sub-state level politicians may of course also act corruptly, perhaps as they see opportunities to enrich themselves or their allies, or may be as these politicians still maintain links with state-wide leaders who have recently empowered them. For discussion of these points see A. Shleifer and R. W. Vishny (1993), 'Corruption', *Quarterly Journal of Economics*, 108 (3): 599–617; J. Huther and A. Shah (2000), *Anti-Corruption Policies and Programmes: A Framework for Evaluation* (Washington D.C.: World Bank, Policy Research Working Paper 2501); R. Fisman and R. Gatti (2002), 'Decentralization and corruption: Evidence across countries', *Journal of Public Economics*, 83 (3): 325–345.

72   T. Ninua (2011), 'Kenya champions open data in Africa', *Space for Transparency, TI Blog*, available on http://blog.transparency.org/2011/07/15/kenya-champions-open-data-in-africa/, viewed on 6 January 2012.

73   N. Ahmed (2010), p.45.

74   'Bangladesh's corruption image slightly better', *The Daily Star*, 3 December 2011, available at http://www.thedailystar.net/newDesign/news-details.php?nid=212619, viewed on 29 December 2011.

Chapter 4   South Korea and Poland: Tough Talk, Small Steps, Contested Outcomes

1   See M. T. Rock and H. Bennett (2004), 'The comparative politics of corruption: Accounting for the East Asian paradox in empirical studies of corruption', *World Development*, 32 (6): 999–1017; N. Ali (2010), *The Coexistence of Corruption and Economic Growth in East Asia: Miracle or*

Alarm, available at http://www.apeaweb.org/confer/hk10/papers/ali_n.pdf, viewed on 25 August 2012.

2   For more information on the data sources used here, see http://info.world-bank.org/governance/wgi/pdf/cc.pdf, viewed on 28 December 2011.

3   A. Shah and M. Schacter (2004), 'Combating corruption: Look before you leap', *Finance and Development*, 41 (4): 42.

4   J-S. You (2009), 'Is South Korea succeeding in controlling corruption?', APSA Meeting, Toronto, 3–6 September, p.1.

5   M. Johnston (2005b), *Syndromes of Corruption* (Cambridge: CUP), pp.89–93.

6   M. Johnston (2005b), p.89.

7   Estimates of the volume of these contributions vary considerably, although Woo makes well-founded claims that in the 1980s and early 1990s the chaebols were giving upwards of 20 per cent of their net profits to politicians and their causes as part of political process. See J-E. Woo (1991), *Race to the Swift: State and Finance in Korean Industrialisation* (New York: Columbia University Press), p.9.

8   See P. J. Soo (1992), *Can Decentralization Policy Constrain the Leviathan?* (Pittsburgh: University of Pittsburgh, Ph.D. Dissertation).

9   See P. J. Soo (1992).

10 See D. Steinberg (2000), 'Korean politics: The new and old', in *KEIA* (ed.) *The Two Koreas in 2000: Sustaining Recovery and Seeking Reconciliation* (Washington, D.C.: KEIA), p.216.

11 V. Bhargava and E. Bolongaita (2004), *Challenging Corruption in Asia: Case Studies and a Framework for Action* (Washington D.C.: World Bank), p.135. See also H. Koo (1993), 'Strong state and contentious society', in H. Koo (ed.) *State and Society in Contemporary Korea* (Ithaca: Cornell University Press), pp.231–249.

12 V. Bhargava and E. Bolongaita (2004), p.135 and p.138.

13 M. Johnston (2005b), p.107.

14 M. Johnston (2005b), p.103. See also T. Y. Kong (1996), 'Corruption and its institutional foundations: The experience of Korea', *Institute of Development Studies Bulletin*, 7 (2): 48–55.

15 M. Johnston (2005b), p.103.

16 K. P. Suk (2007), 'Building national integrity through corruption eradication in South Korea', *International Public Management Review*, 8 (2): 139.

17 V. Bhargava and E. Bolongaita (2004), p.135.

18 For more information on this see K. P. Suk (2007), p.140.

19 K. P. Suk (2007), p.142.

20 For a discussion of these, see V. Bhargava and E. Bolongaita (2004), p.151.

21 Transparency International (2001), *Global Corruption Report 2001*(Berlin: Transparency International).

22 V. Bhargava and E. Bolongaita (2004), p.151.

23 J. S. Quah (2007), *National Integrity Report: Transparency International Regional Overview Report East and South East Asia, 2006* (Berlin: Transparency International), p.6.

24 S. Y. Kim (2005), 'Review on assessing effectiveness of integrity and anti-corruption measures in the Korean public service', in *Public Sector Integrity: A Framework for Assessment* (Paris: Organisation for Economic Cooperation and Development), pp.130–131.

25 Transparency International (2006), *National Integrity Systems Country Study Report: Korea* (Berlin: Transparency International), p.10 and p.15.

26 J. S. Quah (2007), p.10.

27 For more on this see J. S. Quah (2008), *Combating Corruption in the Asia-Pacific Countries: What do We Know and What Needs to be Done?*, paper presented at the Asia-Pacific Governance Institute's Conference on 'The Many Faces of Public Management Reform in the Asia-Pacific' in Bangkok, Thailand 7–9 July, available at http://www.jonstquah.com/images/Corruption_Paper_Bangkok_Conference_2008[1].pdf.

28 'South Korea revamps Anti-Corruption Agencies but fails to eliminate significant loopholes' (2010), *Global Integrity Report* 2009 (Washington D.C.: Global Integrity). See http://report.globalintegrity.org, p.1.

29 World Bank (undated), 'Korean pact on anti-corruption and transparency', available on http://info.worldbank.org/etools/antic/detail.asp?ID=12, viewed on 27 August 2012.

30 Council for the Korean Pact on Anti-Corruption and Transparency (2007), *K-Pact 2007 Annual Report* (Seoul: Council for the Korean Pact on Anti-Corruption and Transparency), p.3. Available on http://www.unglobal-compact.org/system/attachments/3124/original/COP.pdf?1262614878, viewed on 25 August 2012.

31 Global Integrity Report (2010), p.1.

32 Global Integrity Report (2010), p.1.

33 C. Moon (2010), 'South Korea in 2009: From setbacks to reversal', *Asian Survey*, 50 (1), Jan/Feb: 57–58.

34 Quoted in C. Oliver and S. Jung-a (2012), 'S. Korea president says corruption ʼrampant"', *Financial Times*, 13 June.

35 'South Korean President apologises for corruption scandals', *New York Times*, 24 July.

36 K. Olsen (2011), 'Legacy of corruption still exists in South Korea', *Washington Times*, 7 July.

37 S. Mundy (2012), 'Hanwha chairman jailed for four years', *Financial Times*, 16 August.

38 For a brief discussion of just some of these incidences in the 1990s see L. Holmes (1999), *Corruption, Weak States and Economic Rationalism in Central and Eastern Europe*, Paper at the 9th International Anti-Corruption Conference (IACC), 10–15 October 1999, Durban, South Africa. Available athttp://9iacc.org/papers/day1/ws2/dnld/d1ws2_lholmes.pdf

39 For data on this see, for example, K. H. Perdersen and L. Johannsen (2005) *Corruption: Commonality, Causes and Consequences. Comparing 15 Ex-Communist Countries*, paper presented at the 13th NISPA Annual Conference, Moscow.

40 A. Surdej (2005), *Sources of Corruption in Post-Communist Poland* (Bremen: Forschungsstelle Osteuropa, Arbeitspapiere und Materialien, No. 65), p.9.
41 R. Blazszack (2010), 'Has the CBA been effective in tackling corruption in Poland', unpublished BA dissertation thesis, University of Sussex, May, p.9.
42 *National Integrity System Assessment: Poland* (Warsaw: Transparency International and Institute for Public Affairs, 2012), p.2.
43 See W. Kosc (2005), 'Poland, poor Poland', *Transitions Online*, 24 May.
44 R. Blazszack (2010), p.9.
45 A. Surdej (2005), p.5.
46 See Open Society Institute (2002), *Monitoring the EU Accession Process: Corruption and Anti-Corruption Policy* (New York: OSI), p.406.
47 P. Heywood and J-H. Meyer-Sahling (2008), *Corruption Risks and the Management of the Ministerial Bureaucracy in Poland* (Warsaw: Ernst and Young), p.5.
48 C. McManus-Czubinska, W. L. Miller, R. Markowski and J. Wasilewski (2004), 'Why is corruption in Poland "a serious cause for concern"?', *Crime, Law and Social Change*, 41: 113.
49 Commission of the European Communities (2002a), *2002 Regular Report on Poland's Progress Towards Accession* (Brussels: European Commission), 9 October.
50 Commission of the European Communities (2002b), *Towards the Enlarged Union: Strategy Paper* (Brussels, 9 October) p.65. See also C. McManus-Czubinska, W. L. Miller, R. Markowski and J. Wasilewski (2004), 107–132.
51 For more analysis of this period see Anti-Corruption Working Group (2001), *Assumptions of Poland's Anti-Corruption Strategy* (Warsaw: Anti-Corruption Working Group/World Bank).
52 K. Gadowska (2010), 'National and international anti-corruption efforts: The case of Poland', *Global Crime*, 11 (2): 171–182.
53 K. Gadowska (2010), p.178.
54 Batory Foundation (2011), *Anti-Corruption Policy* (Warsaw: Batory Foundation), p.3.
55 National Integrity System Assessment: Poland (2012), p.3.
56 Batory Foundation (2010), *How to Fight Corruption? Principles for Developing and Implementing an Anti-Corruption Strategy in Poland* (Warsaw: Batory Foundation), p.9.
57 Batory Foundation (2011), p.4.
58 Batory Foundation (2011), p.5.
59 P. Heywood and J-H. Meyer-Sahling (2008), p.26.
60 A. Szczerbiak (2007), '"Social Poland" defeats "Liberal Poland"? The September–October 2005 Polish parliamentary and presidential elections', *Journal of Communist Studies and Transition Politics*, 23 (2): 203.
61 A. Szczerbiak (2007), p.212.
62 P. Heywood and J-H. Meyer-Sahling (2008), p.5.
63 For more on this see P. Heywood and J-H. Meyer-Sahling (2008), p.71.

64 J-H. Meyer-Sahling and T. Veen (2012), 'Governing the post-communist state: Government alternation and senior civil service politicisation in Central and Eastern Europe', *East European Politics*, 28 (1): 9.

65 Batory Foundation (2011), pp.5–6.

66 Batory Foundation (2010), p.23.

67 K. Gadowska (2010), p.195.

68 Ernst & Young (2010), *Driving Ethical Grown – New Markets, New Challenges* (Warsaw: Report on the Global Fraud Survey).

69 Batory Foundation (2011), p.5.

70 Batory Foundation (2011), pp.6–7.

71 National Integrity System Assessment: Poland (2012), p.3.

72 National Integrity System Assessment: Poland (2012), p.5.

73 'New agriculture minister appointed in wake of corruption scandal', *Warsaw Business Journal*, 6 August 2012. Available on http://www.wbj.pl/article-59992-new-agriculture-minister-appointed-in-wake-of-corruption-scandal.html, viewed on 16 September 2012.

74 See A. Shah and M. Schacter (2004), p.42.

Chapter 5 Germany and the UK: The Slow and Winding Road to Reform

1 For a detailed comparison of corruption across the western world, see the individual chapters in M. J. Bull and J. Newell (eds) (2003) *Corruption in Contemporary Politics* (Basingstoke: Palgrave).

2 For analysis of Britain in the 1990s see F. F. Ridley and A. Doig (eds) (1995), *Sleaze: Politicians, Private Interests and Public Reaction* (Oxford: OUP). For the specifics of Back to Basics see A. Doig (2001), 'Sleaze: Picking up the threads or "back to basics" scandals', *Parliamentary Affairs*, 54: 260–275. For more on the Flick Affair, see C. Landfried (1994), *Parteifinanzen und politische Macht* (Baden-Baden: Nomos).

3 For the British case see H. Tumber (2004), 'Scandal and media in the United Kingdom: From Major to Blair', *American Behavioural Scientist*; 47 (8): 1122–1137. For the German case C. Clemens (2000); 'A legacy reassessed: Helmut Kohl and the German party finance affair', *German Politics*, 9 (2): 25–50.

4 For more on scandals and their history, see J. Garrard and J. Newell (2006), *Scandals in Past and Contemporary Politics* (Manchester: MUP); J. Thompson (2000), *Political Scandal: Power and Visibility in the Media Age* (London: Polity).

5 See http://info.worldbank.org/governance/wgi/faq.htm#14, viewed on 26 September 2012.

6 The most consistently vocal and long-standing opponent of this thesis remains Hans Herbert von Arnim. See for example H. H. von Arnim (1997), *Fetter Bauch regiert nicht gern. Die politische Klasse – selbstbezogen und abgehoben* (Munich: Kindler); H. H. von Arnim (2001a), *Das System. Die Machenschaften der Macht* (Munich: Droemer); for an English

language version see H. H. von Arnim (2001b), *Institutionalized Political Unaccountability and Political Corruption*, available at http://www.spea.indiana.edu/tac/colloquia/2001/pdf/van%20Arnim.pdf, viewed on 24 August 2012.

7   U. von Alemann (2002), 'Party finance, party donations and corruption: The German case', in D. Della Porta and S. Rose-Ackermann (eds) *Corrupt Exchanges: Empirical Themes in the Politics and Political Economy of Corruption* (Baden: Baden: Nomos), p.112.

8   T. Eschenburg (1970), 'The decline of bureaucratic ethos in the federal republic', in A. J. Heidenheimer (ed.) *Political Corruption: Readings in Comparative Analysis* (New York: Holt, Rinehart and Winston), p.259.

9   P. Noack (1985), *Korruption – die andere Seite der Macht* (Munich: Kindler), p.113.

10 R. Abdelal, R. Di Tella and J. Schlefer (2008), *Corruption in Germany: Managing Germany's Largest Corruption Scandal* (Boston, Mass: Harvard Business School), p.2.

11 For more on the Siemens case see M. Esterl (2006), 'Ethics hurdle: Corruption scandal at Siemens may derail restructuring drive', *Wall Street Journal*, 18 December. For more on the Volkswagen case see S. Power and M. Karnitschnig (2005), 'Risky business: VW's woes mount amid claims of sex junkets for union chiefs', *Wall Street Journal*, 17 November.

12 Transparency International Germany (2012), *National Integrity System Report* (Berlin: TI), p.6.

13 Transparency International Germany (2012), p.6.

14 For more on this see M. Möhrenschlager (2007), 'Der strafrechtliche Schutz gegen Korruption', in D. Dölling (ed.) *Handbuch der Korruptionsprävention* (Munich: Verlag C. H. Beck), pp.377–561.

15 See Transparency International Germany (2012), p.24.

16 S. Wolf (2006), 'Modernization of the German anti-corruption criminal law by international legal provisions', *German Law Journal*, 7 (9): 785. For more on the 1999 laws see F. Zieschang (1999), 'das Eu-Bestechungsgesetz und das Gesetz zur Bekämpfung internationaler Bestechung', *njw*, pp. 105–107.

17 T. M. Funk and J. A. Dance (2012), 'Germany's increasingly robust anti-corruption efforts', *Litigation*, 38 (3), Spring: 1.

18 S. Wolf (2006), p.792.

19 See for example 'German CEOs urge lawmakers to step up action against corruption', *United Nations Office on Drugs and Crime*, 16 August 2012. Available at http://www.unodc.org/unodc/en/frontpage/2012/August/german-ceos-urge-lawmakers-to-step-up-action-against-corruption.html, viewed on 19 August 2012.

20 See for example 'Germany's ruling CDU rejects U.N. corruption pact', *Reuters*, 9 August 2012. Available at http://uk.reuters.com/article/2012/08/09/uk-germany-corruption-idUKBRE8780WK20120809, viewed on 24 August 2012.

21 Transparency International Germany (2012), p.7.

22   R. Hornung (2010), 'Prosecution of corruption: The Baden-Wurttemberg Example', in *Proceedings of the Seminar: Effective Means of Investigation and Prosecution of Corruption* (Bucharest: National Anti-Corruption Directorate of Romania), p.45.

23   Transparency International Germany (2012), p.28.

24   N. Lord (2011), *Regulating Transnational Corporate Bribery in the UK and Germany* (Cardiff: PhD, Cardiff University), pp.131–132.

25   N. Behnke (2002), 'A Nolan Committee for the German ethics infrastructure?', *European Journal of Political Research*, 41: 678.

26   S. Wolf (2006), p.792.

27   See D. Clark, (2000), 'Public service reform: A comparative West European perspective', *West European Politics*, 23: 27.

28   See also N. Behnke (2002), pp.678–679.

29   Transparency International Germany (2012), p.36.

30   Transparency International Germany (2012), pp.36–37.

31   C. Dougherty (2007), 'Prosecutions of business corruption soar in Germany', *New York Times*, 15 February. See also S. Rubenfeld (2011), 'Germany's anti-bribery efforts get high marks from OECD', *Wall Street Journal*, 23 March.

32   T. M. Funk and J. A. Dance (2012), p.1.

33   These range from a number of politicians plagiarising their PhD theses, to the resignation of the Federal President on account of practices that many regarded as corrupt. See for example H. Pidd (2012), 'German President and Merkel ally resigns in corruption scandal', *Guardian*, 17 February; 'Zu Guttenberg resigns: Teflon no more' (2011), *The Economist*, 1 March.

34   A. Adonis (1997), 'The UK: Civic virtue put to the test', in D. Della Porta and Y. Meny (eds) *Democracy and Corruption in Europe* (London: Pinter), p.103.

35   Transparency International UK (2011), *National Integrity System Report* (London: TI), p.14.

36   D. Oliver (1997), 'Regulating the conduct of MPs. The British experience of combating corruption', *Political Studies*, 45 (3): 539–540.

37   For an overview of scandals during this period, and the political issues that they threw up, see F. F. Ridley and A. Doig (1995).

38   See A. Doig (2001), pp.360–375.

39   H. Tumber (2004), pp.1127–1128.

40   B. J. O' Toole (2007), 'The framework of ethical compliance in the UK', *Public Policy and Administration*, 22: 113.

41   For more on the institutional machinery developed for overseeing the behaviour of parliamentarians during this period see O. Gay (2004), 'The development of standards machinery in the Commons', in O. Gay and P. Leopold (eds) *Conduct Unbecoming: The Regulation of Parliamentary Behaviour* (London: Politico's), pp.104–105.

42   *Summary of the Nolan Committee's First Report on Standards in Public Life* (1995), available at http://www.archive.official-documents.co.uk/document/parlment/nolan/nolan.htm, viewed on 26 August 2012.

43 See H. Tumber (2004), pp.1127–1129. See also A. Doig (2003), 'Politics and sleaze: Conservative ghosts and Labour's own brand', *Parliamentary Affairs*, 56 (2), April: 322–333.

44 Guardian (2011), 'Six who fell foul of Elizabeth Filkin', dated 26 November 2001, available at http://www.guardian.co.uk/uk/2001/nov/26/houseofcommons.politics3, accessed on 20 September 2012.

45 For more on this see P. Oborne (2007), *The Triumph of the Political Class* (London: Simon & Shuster UK), pp.222–225.

46 P. Seaward (2010), 'Sleaze, old corruption and parliamentary reform: An historical perspective on the current crisis', *The Political Quarterly*, 81 (1), January–March: 39–48.

47 For more on the UK's parliamentary expenses scandal, see A. Kelso (2009), 'Parliament on its knees: MPs' expenses and the crisis of transparency at Westminster', *The Political Quarterly*, 80 (3), July–September: 329–338; M. Bell (2009), *A Very British Revolution: The Expenses Scandal and How to Save Our Democracy* (London: Icon Books).

48 For details on popular perceptions of this episode, see YouGov/Daily Telegraph, fieldwork 14–16 May 2009, http://iis.yougov.co.uk/ extranets/ygarchives/content/pdf/DT-toplines-MAY.pdf, viewed on 20 September 2012.

49 Transparency International UK (2011), p.6.

50 Lord Falconer, 24 March 2003. Quoted in G. Brown (2007), 'Prevention of corruption – UK legislation and enforcement', *Journal of Financial Regulation and Compliance*, 15 (2): 180. Jack Straw, March 2009. Quoted in M. Osajda (2012), *The UK Bribery Act of 2010: Whiter the FCPA* (London: Thomson Reuters), p.4.

51 P. M. Heywood (2012), 'Integrity management and the public service ethos in the UK: Patchwork quilt or threadbare blanket', *International Review of the Administrative Sciences*, 78 (3): 475–477.

52 P. M. Heywood (2012), p.475. See also Transparency International (2004), *National Integrity Systems TI Country Study Report United Kingdom 2004* (London: TI UK), p.63.

53 The number of actual convictions nonetheless remains hard to assess as in 2009, for example, there were 10,090 prosecutions under the Fraud Act alone, yet not all of them were for offences traditionally understood as corruption. See Transparency International UK (2011), p.14.

54 For a detailed explanation of this see G. Brown (2007), pp.181–182.

55 M. Osajda (2012), p.8.

56 See paragraphs 44–47 in the Bribery Act 2010 Guidance available at: http://www.justice.gov.uk/guidance/docs/bribery-act-2010-guidance.pdf, accessed on 20 September 2012.

57 N. Lord (2011), p.116.

58 M. Osajda (2012), p.8.

59 See for example N. Cecil (2011), 'Golf trips ruled illegal under "confusing" Bribery Act', *London Evening Standard*, 11 January. Available at http://www.standard.co.uk/news/golf-trips-ruled-illegal-under-confusing-bribery-act-6554282.html, viewed on 20 September 2012.

C. Woodhouse (2011), 'Bribery law may drive sponsors out of sport, says Formula 1 team', *London Evening Standard*, 13 January. Available at http://www.standard.co.uk/news/bribery-law-may-drive-sponsors-out-of-sport-says-formula-1-team-6555328.html, viewed on 20 September 2012.

60 See G. Rosenberg (2010), 'New UK Bribery Act 2010 – Draconian in theory but is it enforceable in practice?', *Construction Law International*, 5 (3): 19.

61 Transparency International UK (2011), p.7. See also http://www.transparency.org.uk/all-news-releases/167-government-guidance-deplorable-and-will-weaken-bribery-act, viewed on 20 September 2012.

62 Transparency International UK (2011), p.4.

63 Transparency International UK (2011), p.19.

64 For information on one of their most high-profile successes, see 'Insurance broker jailed for bribing Costa Rican officials', *Serious Fraud Office*, Press Release, 26 October 2010, available at http://www.sfo.gov.uk/press-room/latest-press-releases/press-releases-2010/insurance-broker-jailed-for-bribing-costa-rican-officials.aspx, viewed on 20 September 2012.

65 B. Masters (2011), 'Fraud Watchdog weakened by budget cuts', *Financial Times*, 27 March. Available at http://www.ft.com/cms/s/0/8221-aba2-58b5-11e0-9b8a-00144feab49a.html#axzz27W8Z4X4C, viewed on 20 September 2012.

66 See for example R. Wachman and L. Elliott (2010), 'Serious Fraud Office promises crackdown on firms offering bribers abroad', *The Guardian*, 10 October. Available at http://www.guardian.co.uk/law/2010/oct/10/serious-fraud-office-bribery-crackdown, viewed on 20 September 2012.

67 Transparency International UK (2011), p.8.

68 For more on the various BAE Systems corruption cases, see D. Leigh and R. Evans (2008), 'Sources', *The Guardian* 17 February. Available at http://www.guardian.co.uk/world/2007/jun/07/bae18, viewed on 20 September 2012.

Conclusion

1 D. Kaufmann, A. Kraay and M. Mastruzzi (2009), *Governance Matters VIII* (Washington D.C.: World Bank Development Research Group, Policy Research Paper 4978), p.5.

2 E. Durkheim (1938), *The Rules of Sociological Method* (Chicago: The University of Chicago Press).

Bibliography

Abdelal, R., R. Di Tella and J. Schlefer (2008), *Corruption in Germany: Managing Germany's Largest Corruption Scandal* (Boston, Mass: Harvard Business School).

Ades, A. and R. Di Tella (1996), 'The causes and consequences of competition: A review of recent empirical contributions', *IDS Bulletin*, 27 (2): 6–11.

Adonis, A. (1997), 'The UK: Civic virtue put to the test', in D. Della Porta and Y. Meny (eds) *Democracy and Corruption in Europe* (London: Pinter), pp.103–117.

African Peer Review Mechanism (2006), *Country Review Report of the Republic of Kenya* (Midrand, South Africa: African Peer Review Mechanism), available at http://www.polity.org.za/article/aprm-country-review-report-of-the-republic-of-kenya-december-2006-20, viewed on 3 January 2011.

Ahmed, N. (2010), 'Party politics under a non-party caretaker government in Bangladesh: The Fakhruddin interregnum', *Commonwealth and Comparative Politics*, 48 (1): 23–27.

Alesina, A. and G-M. Angeletos (2005), 'Corruption, inequality and fairness', *Journal of Monetary Economics*, 52 (7): 1227–1244.

Ali, N. (2010), *The Coexistence of Corruption and Economic Growth in East Asia: Miracle or Alarm*, available at http://www.apeaweb.org/confer/hk10/papers/ali_n.pdf, viewed on 25 August 2012.

von Alemann, U. (2002), 'Party finance, party donations and corruption: The German case', in D. Della Porta and S. Rose-Ackermann (eds) *Corrupt Exchanges: Empirical Themes in the Politics and Political Economy of Corruption* (Baden: Baden: Nomos), pp.112–127.

Andersson, S. and P. M. Heywood (2009), 'The politics of perception: Use and abuse of Transparency International's approach to measuring corruption', *Political Studies*, 57 (4): 746–767.

Andrews, M. (2010), 'Good government means different things in different countries', *Governance*, 23 (1): 133–160.

Anti-Corruption Working Group (2001), *Assumptions of Poland's Anti-Corruption Strategy* (Warsaw: Anti-Corruption Working Group/World Bank).

Arndt, C. and C. Oman (2006), *Uses and Abuses of Governance Indicators* (Paris: OECD Development Centre Study).

von Arnim, H. H. (1997), *Fetter Bauch regiert nicht gern. Die politische Klasse – selbstbezogen und abgehoben* (Munich: Kindler).

von Arnim, H. H. (2001a), *Das System. Die Machenschaften der Macht* (Munich: Droemer).

von Arnim, H. H. (2001b), *Institutionalized Political Unaccountability and Political Corruption*, available at http://www.spea.indiana.edu/tac/colloquia/2001/pdf/van%20Arnim.pdf, viewed on 24 August 2012.

Batory Foundation (2010), *How to Fight Corruption? Principles for Developing and Implementing an Anti-Corruption Strategy in Poland* (Warsaw: Batory Foundation).

Batory Foundation (2011), *Anti-Corruption Policy* (Warsaw: Batory Foundation).

Bayley, D. H. (1966), 'The effects of corruption in a developing nation', *Western Political Quarterly*, 19 (4): 719–732.

BBC News Online (2009), 'Kenyan anger over corruption job', available at http://news.bbc.co.uk/2/hi/africa/8231252.stm, viewed on 4 January 2012.

BBC News Online (2009), 'Kenyan corruption chief resigns', available at http://news.bbc.co.uk/2/hi/8283103.stm, viewed on 4 January 2012.

Behnke, N. (2002), 'A Nolan Committee for the German ethics infrastructure?', *European Journal of Political Research*, 41: 675–708.

Bell, M. (2009), *A Very British Revolution: The Expenses Scandal and How to Save our Democracy* (London: Icon Books).

Bhargava, V. and E. Bolongaita (2004), *Challenging Corruption in Asia: Case Studies and a Framework for Action* (Washington DC: World Bank).

Blazszack, R. (2010), *Has the CBA been Effective in Tackling Corruption in Poland?*, unpublished BA dissertation thesis, University of Sussex, May.

Blundo, G. and J. P. Olivier de Sardin (2000), 'La corruption comme terrain. Pour une approche socio-anthropologique', in G. Blundo (ed.) *Monnaier les Povoirs. Espaces, Méchanismes et Représentations de la Corruption* (Paris: Presses universitaires de France, nouveux cahiers de l'IUED), pp.21–46.

Bratton, M. and N. van der Walle (1994), 'Neopatrimonial regimes and political transitions in Africa', *World Politics*, 46 (4): 453–489.

Bribery Act (2010), guidance available at http://www.justice.gov.uk/guidance/docs/bribery-act-2010-guidance.pdf, viewed on 20 September 2012.

Brinkerhoff, D. W. and N. P. Kulibaba (1999), *Identifying and Assessing Political Will for Anti-Corruption Efforts* (Washington D.C.: USAID Working Paper, Number 13).

Brown, E. and J. Cloke (2004), 'Neoliberal reform, governance and corruption in the South: Assessing the international anti-corruption crusade', *Antipode*, 36 (2): 272–294.

Brown, G. (2007), 'Prevention of corruption – UK legislation and enforcement', *Journal of Financial Regulation and Compliance*, 15 (2): 180–185.

Brunetti, A. and B. Weder (1998), *A Free Press is Bad News for Corruption* (Basel: Wirtschaftswissenschaftliches Zentrum der Universität Basel, Discussion Paper, Number 9809).

Brunetti, A. and B. Weder (2003), 'A free press is bad news for corruption', *Journal of Public Economics*, 87: 1801–1824.

Buchanan, J., R. Tollison and G. Tullock (eds) (1980), *Toward a Theory of the Rent-Seeking Society* (College Station: Texas A & M Press).

Bull, M. J. and J. Newell (eds) (2003), *Corruption in Contemporary Politics* (Basingstoke: Palgrave).

Bukovansky, M. (2006), 'The hollowness of anti-corruption discourse', *Review of International Political Economy*, 13 (2): 181–209.

Cecil, N. (2011), 'Golf trips ruled illegal under "confusing" Bribery Act', *London Evening Standard*, 11 January, available at http://www.standard.co.uk/news/

golf-trips-ruled-illegal-under-confusing-bribery-act-6554282.html, viewed on 20 September 2012.

Cherotich, L. A. (undated), *Corruption and Democracy in Kenya* (Amsterdam: Netherlands Institute for Multiparty Democracy), available at http://www.nimd.org/documents/C/corruption_and_democracy_in_kenya.pdf, viewed on 3 January 2012.

Clark, D. (2000), 'Public service reform: A comparative West European perspective', *West European Politics*, 23: 25–44.

Clemens, C. (2000); 'A legacy reassessed: Helmut Kohl and the German Party finance affair', *German Politics*, 9 (2): 25–50.

Collingwood, V. (ed.) (undated), *Good Governance and the World Bank*, available at http://www.ucl.ac.uk/dpu-projects/drivers_urb_change/urb_economy/pdf_glob_SAP/BWP_Governance_World%20Bank.pdf, accessed on 1 December 2011.

Commission of the European Communities (2002a), *2002 Regular Report on Poland's Progress Towards Accession* (Brussels: European Commission), 9 October.

Commission of the European Communities (2002b), *Towards the Enlarged Union: Strategy Paper* (Brussels: European Commission), 9 October.

Council for the Korean Pact on Anti-Corruption and Transparency (2007), *K-Pact 2007 Annual Report* (Seoul: Council for the Korean Pact on Anti-Corruption and Transparency).

Daily Star (2009), 'Ensure free flow of info', 8 August, available at http://www.thedailystar.net/newDesign/news-details.php?nid=100432, viewed on 6 January 2012.

Daily Star (2011), 'Bill passed to protect whistleblowers', 7 June, available at http://www.thedailystar.net/newDesign/news-details.php?nid=188979, viewed on 6 January 2012.

Daily Star (2011), 'Bangladesh's corruption image slightly better', 3 December, available at http://www.thedailystar.net/newDesign/news-details.php?nid=212619, viewed on 29 December 2011.

De Sousa, L. (2010), 'Anti-corruption agencies: Between empowerment and irrelevance', *Crime, Law and Social Change*, 53: 5–22.

Doig, A. (1995), 'Good government and sustainable anti-corruption strategies: A role for independent anti-corruption agencies?', *Public Administration and Development*, 15 (2): 151–165.

Doig, A. (2001), 'Sleaze: Picking up the threads or "back to basics" scandals', *Parliamentary Affairs*, 54 (2): 260–275.

Doig, A. (2003), 'Politics and sleaze: Conservative ghosts and Labour's own brand', *Parliamentary Affairs*, 56 (2), April: 322–333.

Doig, A., D. Watt and R. Williams (2007), 'Why developing country anti-corruption agencies fail to develop', *Public Administration and Development*, 27 (3): 251–259.

Doig, A. (2009), 'Markets, management, managed work and measurement: Setting the context for effective anti-corruption commissions', in L. de Sousa, P. Larmour and B. Hindess (eds) *Governments, NGOs and Anti-Corruption: The New Integrity Warriors* (London: Routledge/ECPR Studies in European Political Science).

Dougherty, C. (2007), 'Prosecutions of business corruption soar in Germany', *New York Times*, 15 February.

Downs, A. (1957), *An Economic Theory of Democracy* (New York: Harper and Row).

Durkheim, E. (1938), *The Rules of Sociological Method* (Chicago: The University of Chicago Press).

Economist (2010), 'A chance to improve how Kenya is run', 29 June.

Economist (2011), 'Zu Guttenberg resigns: Teflon no more', 1 March.

Economist (2011), 'Muhammad Yunus and Bangladesh: Forced out', 5 April.

Economist (2011), 'Bangladesh looks back: Misusing the past', 1 August.

Elliott, K. A. (1997), 'Corruption as an international policy problem: Overview and recommendations', in K. A. Elliott (ed.) *Corruption and the Global Economy* (Washington D.C.: Institute for International Economics).

Elliot, K. A. (2002), 'Corruption as an international policy problem', in A. J. Heidenheimer and M. Johnston (eds) *Political Corruption: Concepts and Contexts* (New Brunswick: Transaction Publishers), pp.925–941.

Ernst & Young (2010), *Driving Ethical Growth – New Markets, New Challenges* (Warsaw: Report on the Global Fraud Survey).

Eschenburg, T. (1970), 'The decline of bureaucratic ethos in the Federal Republic', in A. J. Heidenheimer (ed.) *Political Corruption: Readings in Comparative Analysis* (New York: Holt, Rinehart and Winston), pp.259–265.

Esterl, M. (2006), 'Ethics hurdle: Corruption scandal at Siemens may derail restructuring drive', *Wall Street Journal*, 18 December.

Falaschetti, D. and G. Miller (2001), 'Constraining the Leviathan: Moral hazard and credible commitment in constitutional design', *Journal of Theoretical Politics*, 13 (4): 389–411.

Fisman, R. and R. Gatti (2002), 'Decentralization and corruption: Evidence across countries', *Journal of Public Economics*, 83 (3): 325–345.

Fjeldstad, O-H. and J. C. Andvig (2001), *Corruption: A Review of Contemporary Research* (Bergen: CMI Report R).

Fritzen, S. (2003), *The 'Misery' of Implementation: Governance, Institutions and Anti-Corruption in Vietnam*, paper for conference on 'Governance, Institutions and Anti-Corruption in Asia', New Zealand Asia Institute, University of Auckland, April 2003, available at http://goodgovernance.bappenas.go.id/publikasi_CD/cd_penerapan/ref_cd_penerapan/download/unfolder/Governance..anti-corruption.PDF, viewed on 13 December 2011.

Funk, T. M. and J. A. Dance (2012), 'Germany's increasingly robust anti-corruption efforts', *Litigation*, 38 (3), Spring: 1–3.

Gadowska, K. (2010), 'National and international anti-corruption efforts: The case of Poland', *Global Crime*, 11 (2): 171–195.

Gardiner, J. A. (1993), 'Defining corruption', *Corruption and Reform*, 7: 111–124.

Garrard, J. and J. Newell (2006), *Scandals in Past and Contemporary Politics* (Manchester: MUP).

Gathii, J. T. (1999), 'Corruption and donor reforms: Expanding the promises and possibilities of the rule of law as an anti-corruption strategy in Kenya', *Connecticut Journal of International Law*, 14.

Gay, O. (2004), 'The development of standards machinery in the Commons', in O. Gay and P. Leopold (eds) *Conduct Unbecoming: The Regulation of Parliamentary Behaviour* (London: Politico's), pp.91–140.

Gibson, C. (undated), *Governance, Political Science and the Environment*, available at http://www2.bren.ucsb.edu/~gsd/Gibson_Governance_and_political_science.pdf, viewed on 4 January 2012, p.1.

Gillies, D. (1996), 'Human rights, democracy and good governance: Stretching the World Bank's policy frontiers', in J. Griesgraber and B. Gunter (eds) *The World Bank: Lending on a Global Scale* (London: Pluto Press), pp.104–141.

Githongo, J. (2005), 'Report on my findings of graft in the Government of Kenya', available at http://www.africafocus.org/docs06/git0602.php, viewed on 3 January 2011.

Glaeser, E., R. LaPorta, F. Lopez-de-Silanes and A. Shleifer (2004), 'Do institutions cause growth?', *Journal of Economic Growth*, 9 (3): 271–303.

Global Integrity (2010), *Global Integrity Report* 2009 (Washington DC: Global Integrity).

Goel, R. K. and M. A. Nelson (1998), 'Corruption and government size: A disaggregated analysis', *Public Choice*, XCVII: 107–120.

Guardian (2011), 'Six who fell foul of Elizabeth Filkin', dated 26 November 2001, available at http://www.guardian.co.uk/uk/2001/nov/26/houseofcommons.politics3, accessed on 20 September 2012.

Gupta, A. (1995), 'Blurred boundaries: The discourse of corruption, the culture of politics, and the imagined state', *American Ethnologist*, 22 (2): 375–402.

Gurgur, T. and A. Shah (1999), *The Causes of Corruption* (Washington D.C.: World Bank).

Gurgur, T. and A. Shah (2002), 'Localization and corruption: Panacea or Pandora's Box?', in E. Ahmed and V. Tanzi (eds) *Managing Fiscal Decentralization* (London: Routledge), pp.46–67.

Haarhuis, C. K. (2005), *Promoting Anti-Corruption Reforms* (Utrecht: University of Utrecht, PhD thesis).

Harrison, E. (2007), 'Corruption', *Development in Practice*, 17 (4/5): 672–678.

Heidenheimer, A. J., M. Johnston and V. T. LeVine (eds) (1989), *Political Corruption* (New Brunswick: Transaction Publishers).

Hewitt de Alcantara, C. (1998), 'Uses and abuses of the concept of governance', *International Social Science Journal*, 50 (155): 105–113.

Heywood, P. M. (2012), 'Integrity management and the public service ethos in the UK: Patchwork quilt or threadbare blanket', *International Review of the Administrative Sciences*, 78 (3): 474–493.

Heywood, P. M. and I. Krastev (2006), 'Political scandals and corruption', in P. M. Heywood, E. Jones, M. Rhodes and U. Sedelmeier (eds) *Developments in European Politics* (Basingstoke: Palgrave), pp.157–177.

Heywood, P. M. and J-H. Meyer-Sahling (2008), *Corruption Risks and the Management of the Ministerial Bureaucracy in Poland* (Warsaw: Ernst and Young).

Holmes, L. (1999), *Corruption, Weak States and Economic Rationalism in Central and Eastern Europe*, Paper at the 9th International Anti-Corruption

Conference (IACC), 10–15 October 1999, Durban, South Africa, available at http://9iacc.org/papers/day1/ws2/dnld/d1ws2_lholmes.pdf, viewed on 20 September 2012.

Hopkin, J. (2002), 'States, markets and corruption: A review of some recent literature', *Review of International Political Economy*, 9 (3): 574–590.

Hopkin, J. and A. Rodriguez-Pose (2007), '"Grabbing hand" or "helping hand"? Corruption and the economic role of the state', *Governance*, 20 (2): 187–208.

Hornung, R. (2010), 'Prosecution of corruption: The Baden-Wurttemberg example', in *Proceedings of the Seminar: Effective Means of Investigation and Prosecution of Corruption* (Bucharest: National Anti-Corruption Directorate of Romania), pp.45–53.

Hotchkiss, C. (1998), 'The sleeping dog stirs: New signs of life in efforts to end corruption in international business', *Journal of Public Policy and Marketing*, 17 (1): 108–115.

Huntington, S. (1968), *Political Order in Changing Societies* (New Haven: Yale University Press).

Huther, J. and A. Shah (2000), *Anti-Corruption Policies and Programs: A Framework for Evaluation* (Washington D. C.: World Bank, Policy Research Working Paper, 2501).

Iftekharuzzaman (2005), 'Corruption and human insecurity in Bangladesh', paper presented at Transparency International Bangladesh Anti-Corruption Day held in Dhaka, 9th December, available at http://www.ti-bangladesh.org/research/Corruption&HumanSecurity091205.pdf, viewed on 29 December 2011.

Iftekharuzzaman and T. Mahmud (2008), 'Bangladesh', in Transparency International, *Global Corruption Report 2008* (Cambridge: CUP).

Iftekharuzzman and M. S. Hussein (2010), *Integrity Pledge: Participatory Governance through Social Accountability* (Dhaka: Transparency International).

IMF (1996a), *Partnership for Sustainable Global Growth* (Washington D.C.: Interim Committee Declaration, IMF).

IMF (1996b), 'Summary Proceedings of the 51st Annual Meeting of the Board of Governors' (Washington D.C.: IMF).

IMF (1997a) *The Role of the IMF in Governance Issues – Guidance Note* (Washington D.C.: IMF), available at http://www.imf.org/external/np/sec/nb/1997/NB9715.HTM, viewed on 8 December 2011.

IMF (1997b), *IMF Adopts Guidelines Regarding Governance Issues* (Washington D.C.: IMF News Brief, No. 97/15), available at http://www.imf.org/external/np/sec/nb/1997/NB9715.HTM, viewed on 8 December 2011.

IMF (2002), *The IMF's Approach to Promoting Good Governance and Combating Corruption* (Washington D.C.: IMF).

IMF (2003), *IMF and Good Governance: A Factsheet* (Washington D.C.: IMF), available at http://www.imf.org/external/np/exr/facts/gov.htm, viewed on 8 December 2011.

IMF (2005), *The IMF's Approach to Promoting Good Governance and Combating Corruption – A Guide* (New York: IMF). See also http://www.imf.org/external/np/gov/guide/eng/index.htm, viewed on 11 December 2011.

Irish Times (2011), '$47m of donor money stolen in Kenya', 16 June.

Johnson, J. (2007), 'Bangladesh generals plan anti-corruption drive', *Financial Times*, 16 January.

Johnston, M. (1999), 'A brief history of anticorruption agencies', in A. Schedler, L. Diamond and M. F. Plattner (eds) *The Self-restraining State: Power and Accountability in New Democracies* (Boulder, CO: Lynne Rienner), pp.217–226.

Johnston, M. (2005a), 'Measuring the new corruption rankings: Implications for analysis and reform', in A. J. Heidenheimer and M. Johnston (eds) *Political Corruption: Concepts and Contexts* (London: Transaction Publishers), pp.865–884.

Johnston, M. (2005b), *Syndromes of Corruption* (Cambridge: CUP).

Johnston, M. (2006), 'From Thucydides to Mayor Daley: Bad politics, and a culture of corruption', *P.S. Political Science and Politics*, 39 (4): 809–812.

Kaufmann, D. (2005), 'Myths and realities of governance and corruption', in *The Global Competitiveness Report 2005–2006* (New York: World Economic Forum, OUP).

Kaufmann, D. (2009), 'Aid effectiveness and governance: The good, the bad and the ugly', *Development Outreach* (Washington D.C.: World Bank Institute, February): 26–29.

Kaufmann, D. (2010), 'Governance matters 2010: Worldwide governance indicators highlight governance successes, reversals and failures', available at http://www.brookings.edu/opinions/2010/0924_wgi_kaufmann.aspx, viewed on 6 November 2011.

Kaufman, D. and A. Kraay (2008), 'Governance indicators: Where are we, where should we be going?', *The World Bank Research Observer*, 23 (1): 1–30.

Kaufmann, D., A. Kraay and M. Mastruzzi (2007), *The Worldwide Governance Indicators Project: Answering the Critics* (Washington D.C.: World Bank).

Kaufmann, D., A. Kraay and M. Mastruzzi (2009), *Governance Matters VIII* (Washington D.C.: World Bank Development Research Group, Policy Research Paper 4978).

Kaufmann, D., A. Kraay and P. Zoido-Lobatón (1999), *Aggregating Governance Indicators* (Washington D.C.: World Bank, Policy Research Working Paper 2195).

Kelso, A. (2009), 'Parliament on its knees: MPs' expenses and the crisis of transparency at Westminster', *Political Quarterly*, 80 (3): 329–338.

Kenya Anti-Corruption Authority (2000), *National Anticorruption Plan 2000* (Nairobi: KACA).

Khan, M. (1996), 'A typology of corrupt transactions in developing countries', *IDS Bulletin*, 27 (2): 12–21.

Khan, M. (1998), *Administrative Reforms in Bangladesh* (New Delhi: South Asian Publications).

Khan, M. (2010), 'Corruption and governance in South Asia', in *Europa South Asia Yearbook 2009* (London: Europa, unpublished), available at http://eprints.soas.ac.uk/11683/1/Corruption_and_Governance_in_South_Asia_2009.pdf, viewed on 28 December 2011.

Kim, S. Y. (2005), 'Review on assessing effectiveness of integrity and anti-corruption measures in the Korean public service', in OECD, *Public Sector*

Integrity: A Framework for Assessment (Paris: Organisation for Economic Cooperation and Development).

Kibathi, M. (2011), *Immediate Reforms Needed to Change the Image of Kenya Police* (Nairobi: TI Kenya), available at http://tikenya.org/index.php? option=com_docman&task=doc_download&gid=92&Itemid=146, viewed on 4 January 2012.

Klitgaard, R. (1998), 'International cooperation against corruption', *SPAN*, Sept/October: 38–41.

Koo, H. (1993), 'Strong state and contentious society', in H. Koo (ed.) *State and Society in Contemporary Korea* (Ithaca: Cornell University Press), pp.231–249.

Kong, T. Y. (1996), 'Corruption and its institutional foundations: The experience of Korea', *Institute of Development Studies Bulletin*, 7 (2): 48–55.

Kosc, W. (2005), 'Poland, poor Poland', *Transitions Online*, 24 May.

Knack, S. (2007), 'Measuring corruption: A critique of indicators in Eastern Europe and Central Asia', *Journal of Public Policy*, 27 (3): 263–265.

Knox, C. (2009), 'Dealing with sectoral corruption in Bangladesh: Developing citizen involvement', *Public Administration and Development*, 29: 117–132.

Lambsdorff, J. G. (2005a), 'The methodology of the 2005 corruption perceptions index', available on http://www.icgg.org/downloads/CPI_Methodology. pdf, viewed on 6 December 2011.

Lambsdorff, J. G. (2005b), 'Determining trends for perceived levels of corruption' (Passau: University of Passau, Discussion Paper V-38-05).

Landell-Mills, P. (1999), 'Mobilizing civil society to fight corruption in Bangladesh', *World Bank PremNotes*, October, p.30.

Landfried, C. (1994), *Parteifinanzen und politische Macht* (Baden-Baden: Nomos).

Lawson, L. (2009), 'The politics of anti-corruption reform in Africa', *Journal of Modern African Studies*, 47 (1): 73–100.

Leff, N. (1964), 'Economic development through bureaucratic corruption', *American Behavioral Scientist*, 8 (3): 8–14.

Leigh, D. and R. Evans (2008), 'Sources', *The Guardian*, 17 February, available at http://www.guardian.co.uk/world/2007/jun/07/bae18, viewed on 20 September 2012.

Lopez-Claros, A., M. E. Porter and K. Schwab (2005), *Global Competitiveness Report, 2005–2006: Policies Underpinning Rising Prosperity* (Basingstoke: Palgrave Macmillan); IMD (2005), *World Competitiveness Yearbook, 2005* (Lausanne: IMD), available at http://www01.imd.ch/wcc/ranking/, viewed on 7 December 2011.

Lord, N. (2011), *Regulating Transnational Corporate Bribery in the UK and Germany* (Cardiff: PhD, Cardiff University).

Marquette, H. (2003), *Corruption, Development and Politics: The Role of the World Bank* (Basingstoke: Palgrave).

Marquette, H. (2004), 'The creeping politicisation of the World Bank: The case of corruption', *Political Studies*, 52 (3): 413–430.

Masters, B. (2011), 'Fraud watchdog weakened by budget cuts', *Financial Times*, 27 March, available at http://www.ft.com/cms/s/0/8221aba2-58b5-11e0-9b8a-00144feab49a.html#axzz27W8Z4X4C, viewed on 20 September 2012.

Mauro, P. (1995), 'Corruption and growth', *Quarterly Journal of Economics*, 110 (3): 681–712.

Mauro, P. (1997), *Why Worry About Corruption?* (Washington D.C.: IMF, Economic Issues Series, Number 6).

McManus-Czubinska, C., W. L. Miller, R. Markowski and J. Wasilewski (2004), 'Why is corruption in Poland "a serious cause for concern"?', *Crime, Law and Social Change*, 41 (2): 107–132.

Meyer-Sahling, J-H. and T. Veen (2012), 'Governing the post-communist state: Government alternation and senior civil service politicisation in Central and Eastern Europe', *East European Politics*, 28 (1): 1–19.

Michael, B. (2004), 'The rapid rise of the anti-corruption industry', *Local Governance Brief* (Budapest: Open Society Institute).

Michael, B. (2007), *The Rise and Fall of the Anti-Corruption Industry: Toward Second Generation Anti-Corruption Reforms in Central and Eastern Europe* (Paris: France).

Michael, B. and D. Bowser (2009), *The Evolution of the Anti-Corruption Industry in the Third Wave of Anti-Corruption Work* (New York: Columbia University).

Miller-Adams, M. (1999), *The World Bank: New Agendas in a Changing World* (London: Routledge).

Möhrenschlager, M. (2007), 'Der strafrechtliche Schutz gegen Korruption', in D. Dölling (ed.) *Handbuch der Korruptionsprävention* (Munich: Verlag C. H. Beck), pp.377–561.

Momen, M. (2009), 'Bangladesh in 2008: Déjà vu again or a return to democracy?', *Asian Survey*, 49 (1): 66–73.

Moon, C. (2010), 'South Korea in 2009: From setbacks to reversal', *Asian Survey*, 50 (1), Jan/Feb: 57–58.

Moroff, H. and D. Schmidt-Pfister (2010), 'Anti-corruption movements, mechanisms and machines – an introduction', *Global Crime*, 11 (2): 89–98.

Mullei, C. and A. Mullei (2000), 'Corruption in the court system', in A. Mullei (ed.), *The Link Between Corruption and Poverty: Lessons from Kenya Case Studies* (Nairobi: African Centre for Economic Growth).

Mundy, S. (2012), 'Hanwha chairman jailed for four years', *Financial Times*, 16 August.

Mungiu-Pippidi, A. (2006), 'Corruption: Diagnosis and treatment', *Journal of Democracy*, 17 (3): 86–99.

Mutonyi, J. P. (2002), 'Fighting corruption: Is Kenya on the right track?, *Police Practice & Research, An International Journal*, 3 (1): 21–39.

National Integrity System Assessment: Poland (2012), (Warsaw: Transparency International and Institute for Public Affairs).

New York Times (2012), 'South Korean President apologises for corruption scandals', 24 July.

Ninua, T. (2011), 'Kenya champions open data in Africa', *Space for Transparency, TI Blog*, available on http://blog.transparency.org/2011/07/15/kenya-champions-open-data-in-africa/, viewed on 6 January 2012.

Noack, P. (1985), *Korruption – die andere Seite der Macht* (Munich: Kindler).

Norris, P. (2010), 'Measuring governance', in M. Bevir (ed.) *Sage Handbook of Governance* (London: Sage), pp.411–457.

Nye, J. S. (1967), 'Corruption and political development: A cost-benefit analysis', *American Political Science Review*, 61 (2): 417–427.

Oborne, P. (2007), *The Triumph of the Political Class* (London: Simon & Schuster UK).

OECD (1997), *OECD Convention on Combating Bribery of Foreign Public Officials in International Business Transactions* (Paris: OECD).

OECD (2007), *Glossary of Statistical Terms*, available at http://stats.oecd.org/glossary/detail.asp?ID=7236, accessed on 13 December 2011; UNESCAP (2011), *What is Good Governance?* (New York: United Nations).

Ogwang, L. V. O. (2007), *Rethinking Kenya's Anti-Corruption Strategies: Lessons from Botswana* (Pretoria: University of Pretoria).

Oliver, C. and S. Jung-a (2012), 'S. Korea president says corruption "rampant"', *Financial Times*, 13 June.

Oliver, D. (1997), 'Regulating the conduct of MPs: The British experience of combating corruption', *Political Studies*, 45 (3): 539–540.

Olsen, K. (2011), 'Legacy of corruption still exists in South Korea', *Washington Times*, 7 July.

Open Society Institute (2002), *Monitoring the EU Accession Process: Corruption and Anti-Corruption Policy* (New York: OSI).

Osajda, M. (2012), *The UK Bribery Act of 2010: Whiter the FCPA?* (London: Thomson Reuters).

Otieno, G. (2005), 'The NARC's anti-corruption drive in Kenya: Somewhere over the rainbow?' *African Security Review*, 14 (2): 69–79.

O'Toole, B. J. (2007), 'The framework of ethical compliance in the UK', *Public Policy and Administration*, 22: 109–127.

Palmer, A. (2011), 'A new future for Kenya: Reforming a culture of corruption', *Harvard International Review*, 32 (4).

Perdersen, K. H. and L. Johannsen (2005), *Corruption: Commonality, Causes and Consequences. Comparing 15 Ex-Communist Countries*, paper presented at the 13th NISPA Annual Conference, Moscow.

Perry, P. (1997), *Political Corruption and Political Geography* (Aldershot: Ashgate).

Philp, M. (2006), 'Modelling political corruption in transition', in U. von Alemann (ed.) *Dimensionen politischer Korruption. Beiträge zum Stand der internationalen Forschung* (Wiesbaden: VSVerlag für Sozialwissenschaften), pp.91–108.

Philp, M. (1997), 'Defining political corruption', *Political Studies*, 45 (3): 436–462.

Pidd, H. (2012), 'German President and Merkel ally resigns in corruption scandal', *Guardian*, 17 February.

Pieth, M. (1997), 'Contributions of industrialised countries in the prevention of corruption: The example of the OECD', speech given at the 8th International Anti-Corruption Conference, 7–11 September, available at http://iacconference.org/documents/8th_iacc_workshop_Contribution_of_Industrialised_Countries_in_the_Prevention_of_Corruption_The_Example_of_the_OECD.pdf, viewed on 8 December 2011.

Polity IV (2011), *Polity IV Country Report 2010: Kenya*, available at http://systemicpeace.org/polity/Kenya2010.pdf, viewed on 3 January 2012.

Power, S. and M. Karnitschnig (2005), 'Risky business: VW's woes mount amid claims of sex junkets for union chiefs', *Wall Street Journal*, 17 November.

Quah, J. S. T. (1999), 'Comparing anti-corruption measures in Asian countries: Lessons to be learnt', *Asian Review of Public Administration*, XI (2), July–December: 71–90.

Quah, J. S. T. (2007), *National Integrity Report: Transparency International Regional Overview Report East and South East Asia, 2006* (Berlin: Transparency International).

Quah, J. S. T. (2008), *Combating Corruption in the Asia-Pacific Countries: What do We Know and What Needs to be Done?*, paper presented at the Asia-Pacific Governance Institute's Conference on 'The Many Faces of Public Management Reform in the Asia-Pacific' in Bangkok, Thailand 7–9 July, available at http://www.jonstquah.com/images/Corruption_Paper_Bangkok_Conference_2008[1].pdf.

Reuters (2012), 'Germany's ruling CDU rejects U.N. corruption pact', 9 August, available at http://uk.reuters.com/article/2012/08/09/uk-germany-corruption-idUKBRE8780WK20120809, viewed on 24 August 2012.

Ridley, F. F. and A. Doig (eds) (1995) *Sleaze: Politicians, Private Interests and Public Reaction* (Oxford: OUP).

Riley, S. (1998), 'The political economy of anti-corruption strategies in Africa', in M. Robinson (ed.) *Corruption and Development* (London: Frank Cass).

Rock, M. T. and H. Bennett (2004), 'The comparative politics of corruption: Accounting for the East Asian paradox in empirical studies of corruption', *World Development*, 32 (6): 999–1017.

Roberts, H. (2003), *Political Corruption in and Beyond the Nation State* (London: Routledge).

Roberts, J. and S. Fagernäs (2004), *Why is Bangladesh Outperforming Kenya? A Comparative Study of Growth and Its Causes since the 1960s* (London: Overseas Development Institute, ESAU Working Paper 5).

Rosenberg, G. (2010), 'New UK Bribery Act 2010 – Draconian in theory but is it enforceable in practice?', *Construction Law International*, 5 (3): 19.

Rose-Ackerman, S. (1978), *Corruption: A Study in Political Economy* (New York: Academic Press).

Rose-Ackerman, S. (1999), *Corruption and Government: Causes, Consequences and Reform* (Cambridge: CUP).

Rothstein, B. (2011), 'Anti-corruption: The indirect "big bang" approach', *Review of International Political Economy*, 18 (2): 228–250.

Rowley, C., R. Tollison and G. Tullock (eds) (1989), *The Political Economy of Rent-Seeking* (Boston: Kluwer).

Rubenfeld, S. (2011), 'Germany's anti-bribery efforts get high marks from OECD', *Wall Street Journal*, 23 March.

Sampson, S. (2007), *Can the World Bank Do the Right Thing? When Anti-Corruption Movements Become Anti-Corruption Budget Lines*, paper for American Anthropological Association annual meeting, Washington D.C., November 2007, available at http://www.lunduniversity.lu.se/o.o.i.s?id=12683&postid=1146197, viewed on 6 December 2011.

Sampson, S. (2008), 'Corruption and anti-corruption in South-East Europe: Landscapes and sites', in L. de Sousa, P. Larmour and B. Hindess (eds) *Governments, NGOs and Anti-Corruption: The New Integrity Warriors* (London: Routledge).

Sampson, S. (2010), 'Diagnostics: Indicators and transparency in the anti-corruption industry', in S. Jansen, E. Schroeter and N. Stehr (eds) *Transparenz: multidisziplinaere Durchsichten durch Phoenomene und Theorien des Undurchsichtigen* (Wiesbaden: VS Verlag), pp.97–111.

Saxton, J. (1999), *Can IMF Lending Promote Corruption?* (Washington D.C.: US Congress, Joint Economic Committee).

Schiller, C. (2000), *Improving Governance and Fighting Corruption: An IMF Perspective* (Washington D.C.: IMF, Fiscal Affairs Department).

Schmidt, D. (2007) 'Anti-corruption: What do we know? Research on preventing corruption in the post-communist world', *Political Studies Review*, 5 (2): 202–232.

Seaward, P. (2010), 'Sleaze, old corruption and parliamentary reform: An historical perspective on the current crisis', *The Political Quarterly*, 81 (1), January–March: 39–48.

Serious Fraud Office (2010), 'Insurance broker jailed for bribing Costa Rican officials', Press Release, 26 October, available at http://www.sfo.gov.uk/press-room/latest-press-releases/press-releases-2010/insurance-broker-jailed-for-bribing-costa-rican-officials.aspx, viewed on 20 September 2012.

Shah, A. (2007), 'Tailoring the fight against corruption to country circumstances', in A. Shah (ed.) *Performance Accountability and Combating Corruption* (Washington D.C.: World Bank), pp.233–254.

Shah, A. and M. Schachter (2004), 'Combating corruption: Look before you leap', *Finance and Development*, 41 (4): 40–43.

Shlefier, A. and R. Vishny (1993), 'Corruption', *Quarterly Journal of Economics*, 108 (3): 599–617.

Smilov, D. (2010), 'Anticorruption agencies: Expressive, constructivist and strategic uses', *Crime, Law and Social Change*, 53 (1): 67–77.

Smith, B. C. (2007), *Good Governance and Development* (Basingstoke: Palgrave).

Soo, P-J. (1992), *Can Decentralization Policy Constrain the Leviathan?* (Pittsburgh: University of Pittsburgh, Ph.D. Dissertation).

Stapenhurst, R. (2000), *The Media's Role in Curbing Corruption* (Washington D.C.: World Bank).

Steinberg, D. (2000), 'Korean politics: The new and old', in *KEIA* (ed.) *The Two Koreas in 2000: Sustaining Recovery and Seeking Reconciliation* (Washington, D.C.: KEIA).

Stiglitz, J. (2002), *Globalization and its Discontents* (London: Allen Lane).

Suk, K-P. (2007), 'Building national integrity through corruption eradication in South Korea', *International Public Management Review*, 8 (2): 139–142.

Surdej, A. (2005), *Sources of Corruption in Post-Communist Poland* (Bremen: Forschungsstelle Osteuropa, Arbeitspapiere und Materialien, No. 65).

Svensson, J. (2005), 'Eight questions about corruption', *Journal of Economic Perspectives*, 19 (3): 19–42.

Szczerbiak, A. (2007), '"Social Poland" defeats "Liberal Poland"? The September–October 2005 Polish parliamentary and presidential elections', *Journal of Communist Studies and Transition Politics*, 23 (2): 203–212.

Szeftel, M. (1998), 'Misunderstanding African politics: Corruption and the governance agenda', *Review of African Political Economy*, 76: 221–240.

Tanzi, V. (1994), *Corruption, Government Activities and Markets* (Washington D.C.: IMF, Working Paper 94/99).

Tanzi, V. (1998), *Corruption Around the World: Causes, Consequences, Scope and Cures* (Washington D.C.: IMF, Working Paper 98/63).

Tanzi, V. (2000a), 'Corruption, growth and public finances', *IMF Working Papers* (Washington D.C.: IMF, Working Paper 00/182).

Tanzi, V. (2000b), *Policies, Institutions and the Dark Side of Economics* (Cheltenham: Edward Elgar).

Tanzi, V. and H. Davoodi (1998), *Roads to Nowhere: How Corruption in Public Investment Hurts Growth* (Washington D.C.: IMF, Economic Issues Series, number 12).

Thomas, M. A. (2010), 'What do the worldwide governance indicators measure', *European Journal of Development of Research*, 22 (1): 31–54.

Thompson, J. (2000), *Political Scandal: Power and Visibility in the Media Age* (London: Polity).

Thompson, T. and A. Shah (2005), *Transparency International's Corruption Perceptions Index: Whose Perceptions are They Anyway?* (Washington D.C.: World Bank).

Transparency International (2001), *Global Corruption Report 2001* (Berlin: Transparency International).

Transparency International (2004), *National Integrity Systems TI Country Study Report United Kingdom 2004* (London: TI UK).

Transparency International (2006), *National Integrity Systems Country Study Report: Korea* (Berlin: Transparency International).

Transparency International (2011), *Transparency International Corruption Perceptions Index (CPI) 2011. A Short Methodological Note*, available at http://www.transparency.ie/sites/default/files/Short%20methodological%20note%20CPI%202011%2025%20nov%2011.pdf, accessed on 6 December 2011.

Transparency International Bangladesh (2010), *Annual Report 2009* (Dhaka: Transparency International).

Transparency International Bangladesh (2011a), *Annual Report 2010* (Dhaka: Transparency International).

Transparency International Bangladesh (2011b), *Making the Anti-Corruption Commission Effective* (Dhaka: TIB, Policy Brief).

Transparency International Germany (2012), *National Integrity System Report* (Berlin: TI).

Transparency International Kenya (2002), *After KACA What Next? Fighting Corruption in Kenya* (Nairobi: Transparency International-Kenya).

Transparency International UK (2011), *National Integrity System Report* (London: TI).

Treisman, D. (2007), 'What have we learned about the causes of corruption from ten years of cross-national empirical research?', *Annual Review of Political Science*, 10: 211–244.

Tumber, H. (2004), 'Scandal and media in the United Kingdom: From Major to Blair', *American Behavioural Scientist*; 47 (8): 1122–1137.

UNDP (1997), *Governance for Sustainable Human Development* (New York, UNDP). Also available at http://mirror.undp.org/magnet/policy/chapter1. htm#b, accessed on 13 December 2011.

UNDP (2007), *Governance Indicators: A Users' Guide* (Oslo: UNDP, 2nd Edition).

United Nations (1996), *General Assembly Declaration Against Corruption and Bribery in International Commercial Transactions*, Document A/RES/51/191, available at http://www.un.org/documents/ga/res/51/a51r191.htm, accessed on 8 December 2011.

United Nations Office on Drugs and Crime (2012), 'German CEOs urge lawmakers to step up action against corruption', 16 August, available at http://www. unodc.org/unodc/en/frontpage/2012/August/german-ceos-urge-lawmakers-to-step-up-action-against-corruption.html, viewed on 19 August 2012.

Vogl, F. (1998), 'The supply side of global bribery', *Finance and Development*, 35 (2): 55–64.

Wachman, R. and L. Elliott (2010), 'Serious Fraud Office promises crackdown on firms offering bribers abroad', *The Guardian*, 10 October, available at http://www.guardian.co.uk/law/2010/oct/10/serious-fraud-office-bribery-crackdown, viewed on 20 September 2012.

Warsaw Business Journal (2012), 'New agriculture minister appointed in wake of corruption scandal', 6 August, available at http://www.wbj.pl/article-59992-new-agriculture-minister-appointed-in-wake-of-corruption-scandal.html, viewed on 16 September 2012.

Warutere, P. (undated), *Anatomy of a Scandal: Money, Power and the Winded Path of Goldenberg's Deals*, available at http://www.ipocafrica.org/index.php? option=com_content&view=article &id=69&Itemid=68, viewed on 3 January 2012.

Williams, R. (2000), 'Introduction', in R. Williams and A. Doig (eds) *Controlling Corruption* (Cheltenham: Edward Elgar).

Woodhouse, C. (2011), 'Bribery law may drive sponsors out of sport, says Formula 1 team', *London Evening Standard*, 13 January, available at http:// www.standard.co.uk/news/bribery-law-may-drive-sponsors-out-of-sport-says-formula-1-team-6555328.html, viewed on 20 September 2012.

Wolf, S. (2006), 'Modernization of the German anti-corruption criminal law by international legal provisions', *German Law Journal*, 7 (9): 785–792.

Woo, J-E. (1991), *Race to the Swift: State and Finance in Korean Industrialisation* (New York: Columbia University Press).

World Bank (1991), *Managing Development – The Governance Dimension* (Washington D.C.: World Bank).

World Bank (1992), *Governance and Development* (Washington, D.C.: World Bank).

World Bank (1994), *Governance: The World Bank's Experience* (Washington, D.C.: World Bank).

World Bank (2004), *World Bank Anti-Corruption Strategy* (Washington D.C.: World Bank).

World Bank (2007), *Strengthening World Bank Group Engagement on Governance and Anticorruption* (Washington D.C.: World Bank, Joint Ministerial Committee of the Boards of Governors of the Bank and the Fund on the Transfer of Real Resources to Developing Countries).

World Bank (undated), *Helping Countries Combat Corruption: The Role of the World Bank* (Washington D.C.: World Bank), available at http://www1.worldbank.org/publicsector/anticorrupt/corruptn/cor02.htm, viewed on 1 December 2011.

World Bank (undated), 'Korean pact on anti-corruption and transparency', available at http://info.worldbank.org/etools/antic/detail.asp?ID=12, viewed on 27 August 2012.

Wrong, M. (2009), *Our Turn to Eat: The Story of a Kenyan Whistleblower* (New York: Harper).

You, J-S. (2009), 'Is South Korea succeeding in controlling corruption?', APSA Meeting, Toronto, 3–6 September.

YouGov/Daily Telegraph, fieldwork 14–16 May 2009, http://iis.yougov.co.uk/extranets/ygarchives/content/pdf/DT-toplines-MAY.pdf, viewed on 20 September 2012.

Zafarullah, H. and R. Rahman (2008), 'The impaired state: Assessing state capacity and governance in Bangladesh', *International Journal of Public Sector Management*, 21 (7): 739–752.

Zakiuddin, A. (undated), *Corruption in Bangladesh: An Analytical and Sociological Study*, available at http://www.ti-bangladesh.org/docs/research/CorBang1.htm, viewed on 29 December 2011.

Zhong, N. (2010), *The Causes, Consequences and Cures of Corruption: A Review of Issues* (Hong Kong: The Chinese University of Hong Kong), available at http://www.usc.cuhk.edu.hk/PaperCollection/webmanager/wkfiles/7489_1_paper.pdf, viewed on 7 December 2011.

Zieschang, F. (1999), 'Das EU-Bestechungsgesetz und das Gesetz zur Bekämpfung internationaler Bestechung', *NJW*: 105–107.

Index

Adonis, Andrew   105
African Governance Indicators
    (AGI)   19
African Union's Anti-Corruption
    Convention   66
Ahmed, Fakhruddin   56, 59
Al-Yamamah   111
Anglo-Leasing Scandal (Kenya)   64,
    66
Anti-Corruption Agencies (ACAs)
    43, 44, 45, 68, 80, 81–82, 91,
    99, 104–105, 111, 112, 116,
    118, 119–120
Anti-Corruption and Civil Rights
    Commission (ACRC, South
    Korea)   82
Anti-Corruption and Economic
    Crimes Act (ACECA, Kenya)
    66
Anti-corruption industry   12,
    20–22, 29–30, 114
Anti-Corruption Police Unit (ACPU,
    Kenya)   65–66
Anti-Corruption Working Group
    (Poland)   85
Arap-Moi, Daniel   66
Asian Crisis (1997)   71, 79
Athenian Democracy   7
Audit Commission (UK)   111
Awami League (Bangladesh)
    55–56, 59

Back to Basics (UK)   107
BAE Systems   111–112
Bangladesh Nationalist Party (BNP)
    55–56
BASF   105, 112
Blair, Tony   97, 107–108, 111–112
Board of Audit and Inspection (BAI,
    South Korea)   80
Bribe Payers Index (TI)   17, 18

Brooke, Heather   108
Business Environment and
    Enterprise Survey (BEEPS)
    18–19
Buzek, Jerzy   87

Caretaker Government (Bangladesh)
    56–59
Cash for Questions (UK)   106–107
Central Anticorruption Bureau
    (CBA, Poland)   88–89, 91–92,
    118
Chaebols   78, 83, 92, 118
China   50
Chung Sang-mun   83
Citizens' Coalition for Promulgating
    a Corruption Prevention Law
    (South Korea)   80–81
Civic Platform Party (Poland)   89
Clientelism   84, 88
Cold War   1, 14
Committees of Concerned Citizens
    (CCC, Bangladesh)   60–62,
    70
Committee on Standards in Public
    Life (UK)   106–108, 113
Conservative Party (UK)
    Conservative/Lib Dem
        Government   111
    General   107–108
Council of Europe (CoE)   2, 20, 85,
    102, 105
Country Policy and Institutional
    Assessment (CPIA)   42

Decentralisation and Localism Bill
    (UK)   111
Denmark   6, 15
Department for Environment, Food
    and Rural Affairs (DEFRA, UK)
    111

Department of Work and Pensions
(DWP, UK) 111
Developmental Economists 3, 13
Doncaster (local authority, UK) 111

Eigen, Peter 15
Elite cartel corruption 78, 79
Ethics and Anti-Corruption
Commission (EACC, Kenya) 68
European Commission 85
European Union 20, 84, 85, 87

Falconer, Charlie (Lord) 109
Filkin, Elizabeth 108
Financial Intelligence Unit (FIU,
Bangladesh) 56
Finland 6
Flick Affair 93, 100
Foreign Corrupt Practices Act
(FCPA, USA) 26
Freedom of Information
Act (FOI, UK) 108
Kenya 70, 117

G20 countries 42
Garlicki, Miroslaw 89
Githongo, John 67
Global Corruption Barometer
(TI) 17, 18
Global Integrity 83
Goldenberg Affair 64
Greece 8, 42
Grey Web (Poland) 88
Group of States Against Corruption
(GRECO) 103

Hanwha Group 83
Hasina, Sheikh 55, 57, 59, 60
Hyundai 83

Independent Anti-Corruption
Commission (IACC,
Bangladesh) 58–59
Independent Parliamentary
Standards Authority (IPSA,
UK) 4
Indonesia 14, 15

Integrity Pledges 61, 62, 70
International Country Risk Guide
(ICRG) 19
International Criminal Court 67
International Monetary Fund 2, 3,
5, 6, 7, 20, 25, 27, 29, 33, 34, 64
Italy 8, 42

Jago Manush (Bangladesh) 61

Kaczynski, Jaroslaw 88
Kaczynski, Lech 87–88
Kenyan Anti-Corruption Authority
(KACA) 65
Kenyan Anti-Corruption
Commission (KACC) 66–68,
70
Kibaki, Mwai 62, 66, 67
Kim Dae-jung 80–81
Kim Young-sam 80
Kohl, Helmut 94
Korean Pact on Anti-Corruption and
Transparency (K-Pact) 82
Korean Independent Commission
Against Corruption (KICAC)
81–82

Labour Party (UK) 107–108, 109
Lambsdorff, Johann Graf 17
Law and Justice Party (PiS, Poland)
87–90, 117–118, 119
Lean government 5, 31, 32
Lee Myung-bak 83
Lepper, Andrzej 89
London Stock Exchange 110

Major, John 97, 106–107
Merkel, Angela 103
Ministry of Defence (MoD, UK)
111
Money Laundering Prevention Act
(South Korea) 81
Mwau, John 65

National Health Service (NHS, UK)
111
New Zealand 8, 15, 42

Non-Governmental Organisations
    (NGOs)
    in general   20, 22, 26, 38, 59
    in Poland   89
    in South Korea   81, 92, 118
North Korea   15, 49

Odinga, Raila   62
Orange Democratic Movement
    (Kenya)   62
Organisation for Economic
    Co-operation and Development
    (OECD)
    Convention on Combating
        Bribery   26, 85, 102
    definition of corruption   2
    Governance agenda   7, 33
    in General   17, 20, 21, 103, 105
Overseas Anti-Corruption Unit
    (OACU, UK)   111

Park Yeon-cha   83
Parliamentary Expenses Scandal
    (UK)   4, 97, 108–109, 113, 120
Party of National Unity (Kenya)   62
Philippines   14
Public Choice Approach   6, 23–25,
    27–28, 29
Public Officer Ethics Act (Kenya)
    66

Real Name Transactions Act (South
    Korea)   80
Right to Information Act
    (Bangladesh)   60
Ringera, Aaron   67–68, 70
Roh Geon-pyong   83
Roh Moo-hyun   83

Samoobrona (Poland)   89
Samsung   83
Saudi Arabia   49, 111
Schröder, Gerhard   103
Select Committee on Standards and
    Privileges (UK)   107
Serious Fraud Office (SFO, UK)
    110, 111, 112

Serious Organised Crime Agency
    (SOCA, UK)   111
Siemens   100, 105, 112
Singapore   15
Slovakia   88
Somalia   15
Standing Conference of Federal
    State Ministers and Senators
    of the Interior (IMK, Germany)
    102
Straw, Jack   109
Sweden   6

Terrorism   37, 97
Transparency International
    Bangladesh   46, 54, 58, 59,
        60–62, 70
    Bribe Payers' Index   17–18
    Corruption definition   2
    Corruption Perceptions Index
        (TI)   9, 10, 11, 15–18, 29, 46,
        47, 54, 58, 63, 64, 70, 75, 76,
        78, 86, 89, 94, 97, 101, 106,
        117
    General   15, 20
    Germany   101, 103
    Global Corruption Barometer
        17, 18
    Kenya   63, 64
    Poland   86
    South Korea   78, 81
    UK   106, 109, 110, 111
Tusk, Donald   91

UK Bribery Act (UKBA)   99,
    109–110, 112, 113, 119
UK Fraud Act   109
United Nations
    in general   20, 26–27
    United Nations Convention
        against Corruption (UNCAC)
        57, 102, 103, 105
    United Nations Declaration
        against Corruption and
        Bribery in International
        Commercial Transactions
        26

United Nations Development
  Programme (UNDP)   7, 32
United Nations Economic and
  Social Commission for Asia
  and the Pacific (UNESCAP)
  33
Union Parishad (Bangladesh)   62
United States Agency for
  International Development
  (USAID)   21
USA   26, 97, 104

Volkswagen   100

Westminster (local authority, UK)
  111
Whistleblower Act (Bangladesh)
  60
Wolfensohn, James   12, 15, 22,
  23, 28

World Bank
  Approach to tackling corruption
    3, 5, 6, 20, 21, 27, 28–29
  Definition of corruption   2
  in general   17, 28
  Governance agenda   7, 32, 34
  Kenya   64
  Poland   85
World Economic Forum (WEF)   19
World Governance Indicators
  (WGI)   5, 9, 18, 36, 37–45, 46,
  48, 50–52, 70, 72–76, 89, 94–98,
  99, 115, 117, 118

Youth Engagement and Support
  Groups (YES, Bangladesh)   61,
  62, 70
Yunus, Muhammad   59

Zia, Khaleda   55, 57, 58

CPSIA information can be obtained at www.ICGtesting.com
Printed in the USA
LVOW07*1901080814

398224LV00006B/193/P

9 781137 268709